How to Rethink Psychology

Based on the author's forty years of experience in psychology, philosophy, and the social sciences, *How to Rethink Psychology* argues that to understand people we need to know more about their contexts than the dominant modes of thinking and research presently allow. Drawing upon insights from sources as diverse as Freud, CBT, quantum physics, and Zen philosophy, the book offers several fascinating new metaphors for thinking about people and, in doing so, endeavors to create a psychology for the future.

The book begins by discussing the significance of the key metaphor underlying mainstream psychology today – the 'particle' or 'causal' metaphor – and explains the need for a shift towards new 'wave' or 'contextual' metaphors in order to appreciate how individual and social actions truly function. It explores new metaphors for thinking about the relationship between language and reality, and teaches the reader how they might reimagine the processes involved in the act of thinking itself. The book concludes with a consideration of how these new metaphors might be applied to practical methods of research, understanding, and effecting change.

How to Rethink Psychology is important reading for upper-level and postgraduate students and researchers in the fields of social psychology, critical psychology, and the philosophy of psychology, and will especially appeal to those studying behavior analysis and radical behaviorism. It has also been written for the general reading public who enjoy exploring new ideas in science and thinking.

Bernard Gueri … he University of South Australia.

How to Rethink Psychology

New metaphors for understanding people and their behavior

Bernard Guerin

LONDON AND NEW YORK

First published 2016
by Routledge
27 Church Road, Hove, East Sussex BN3 2FA

and by Routledge
711 Third Avenue, New York, NY 10017

Routledge is an imprint of the Taylor & Francis Group, an informa business

British Library Cataloguing in Publication Data
A catalogue record for this book is available from the British Library

Library of Congress Cataloguing in Publication data
Guerin, Bernard, 1957–
How to rethink psychology : new metaphors for understanding people and their behavior / Bernard Guerin.
pages cm
1. Psychology. 2. Thought and thinking. 3. Psycholinguistics. I. Title.
BF121.G84 2016
150.1–dc23
2015007989

ISBN: 978-1-138-91653-1 (hbk)
ISBN: 978-1-138-91654-8 (pbk)
ISBN: 978-1-315-68955-5 (ebk)

Typeset in Times New Roman
by Out of House Publishing
Printed in Great Britain by Ashford Colour Press Ltd.

Contents

Tables

Preface

This book arose from of many years thinking and researching about people and how to understand them. I have adopted and moved on from almost every position, theory, foundation, or paradigm in existence: always learning from them; always trying to grasp what they were desperately and uniquely trying to add before moving on; always taking something away with me. These positions have come from philosophy, psychology, Zen, psychiatry, novels, films, and other media.

This book is not my summation or final, pivotal foundation for thinking about people. Its first words are: "The aim of this book is not to convince you of what I think. The aim is to get you to think differently about people and how they behave than you do now." Like Gilles Deleuze, who lies hidden in the background of this book, the whole point is that life and the world changes and morphs, so there is no certain, secure foundation that we can speak, nor will there be. What you need to learn is how to keep thinking in new ways to keep on top of things. The following is from a Facebook posting I made while in the middle of writing this book:

> While writing a new book I suddenly realize that all my writings have been like the diaries of explorers. I push bravely, ruthlessly sometimes, into the jungle and write to people back home of what I am seeing and experiencing. Most of those back home have no idea what I am saying and are puzzled, or attribute the writing to "too much time in the sun". They safely package what I write about into their own categories and ideas because they cannot see the beauty, freedom and dangers of these new lands. It is not their fault; I barely know what I am seeing let alone how to describe things here. One part of me wants to break it all open and let them see it as I am seeing it; but another part of me wants to leave it alone, turn around and tell them that I was mistaken and it did not

> exist this way – "Go back to your old paradigms!" New ideas, like new worlds, are too precious to hand over to the 'civilized' world. People will only come in, debase the beauty, categorize into submission, and begin to own these lands as their territory. Perhaps, I next think, I will continue to explore and write my diaries, but I will keep them to myself and pretend they were never written. Then I wonder; how many others have been here before me and done the same? There must be secret explorer diaries everywhere …

So it is in this spirit that I would like you to read this book. Do not agree or disagree with everything I write, just learn how to find new ways of thinking about your life and the people you deal with in your life and work. What I do know is that older ways of thinking about people, in common sense, psychology and psychiatry, have colonized with words and made life into static models that are not working well – because our lives are fluid.

So this book is really a self-help, skill-teaching book to teach you some thinking-about-people skills (hence the title). There is also a text appearing to teach you how to analyze real people and situations in their contexts (Guerin, forthcoming). I cannot know or give a basis to all the issues and problems you and the people around you experience; what I hope to do is to give you some skills to approach and handle these issues and problems in new ways that might work better. But they will be your new ways based on your immediate experience, not some worn-out words of mine.

In line with this being a skills-training book, I have not gone along with some reviewers' comments and added discussions and reviews of all my sources with lots of references. If you would like that, look in my last books, which are totally over-referenced and bogged down, and follow the citations outwards from there. I have mentioned my main sources and inspirations in this book, but often these are also novels, films, and watching people in the real world. I would have you do the same.

But most of all, enjoy! Try and stop yourself going into opposition to what I say and try instead to just see if you can think that way – can you even think it? Once you can, you are free to improve, change, debunk, etc. But most of all, enjoy seeing the wonderfully crazy human race in new ways that show that not all humans are crazy really, but they are wonderful!

Reference

Guerin, B. (forthcoming). *Understanding people through social contextual analysis: A practical guide*. Abingdon: Routledge.

Acknowledgements

This book is a culmination of many years, so there are too many people to thank (or even remember). There are also too many authors of novels and film directors to thank them all. There are also too many people I have observed and whose crazy but wonderful human behavior I have thought about to ever thank, even if they did not know I was learning from their actions. So I will generically: thank everyone who has commented on or contributed to my work over the years in a productive or facilitative way, whether favorably or not I do not mind; thank the wonderful authors and directors of creative works that I have learned from; and thank all the people I have observed – thank you for being human.

There are just a few I will mention specifically. First Gui, Vincent, and Marcela for listening to my metaphors and not laughing, and, moreover, contributing to their development. Thanks to Kamelia for reading through an early draft and making great comments which I have incorporated: she was a brute reality check for my writing. Over the longer period I will also single out two special people to thank: the late Frank Herbert for his 'Dune' series of books, which have long given me much food for thought and inspiration, and the late Gilles Deleuze for always thinking ahead. Finally, also many thanks to the staff at Routledge for their belief in this book and their production work.

1 Understanding our own psychology

Alternative ways to think?

The aim of this book is not to convince you of what I think. The aim is to get you to think differently about people and how they behave than you do now. We often read about science and medical topics and learn that we might have been thinking wrongly about them. What if there was no 'Big Bang' that started our universe but a 'Bang' that was only one of a recurring series? What if it turns out that coffee was the most powerful ingredient to combat all forms of cancer (my dream)? What if the Large Hadron Collider machine finds new subatomic particles that do not fit any of the current theories? What if this chair is made up of mostly empty space? What if our bookcase could, with a small probability, suddenly appear in another galaxy and then come back again? What if the Earth is not flat?

Rethinking what we think we know is not new: Sir Isaac Newton treated light as little particles flying in a straight line, but they were later thought of as waves with James Clerk Maxwell; then they were particles again; then they were both particles and waves; and now they are neither particles nor waves. We are used to these new insights and 'turn-around' ideas in news reports, in popular science books, and now on Web news-feeds, and they dazzle us when we have to begin thinking at 180° to what we normally think. Scary and bothersome to some people perhaps, but fun for most of us (for example, Barrow, 2007; Chown, 2007; Hawking, 1988; Matthews, 2005; Penrose, 2010).

What I want to teach you in this book are similar rethinkings or reimaginings, but the problem for you is that I want you to rethink that which is most dear and seemingly true – *how you think about yourself and other people*. The ideas which I will present have been around for a long time. They are not totally new inventions, but they are consistent with all we know about people and all we know about you! They are not science fiction or fantasy. But you will have to try and totally reimagine the ways you think about yourself and others.

Let me give just one example here of the reimagining to get you started. In a later chapter I will suggest that there have been only four ways that people think about the use of language: we say that we use language to *express* things or ideas; we use language to *communicate* ideas; we use language to *refer* to things; or we use language to *represent* things and ideas. This seems sensible enough and this is how we normally talk and think about our uses of language in everyday life. This is also the way scholars talk and think about the use of language. (It is also, not co-incidentally, the way people talk and think about the uses of music – music is said to express, communicate, refer to or represent musical ideas.)

However, when we get to that part of the book, I will be arguing that all these four ways of thinking and talking about language use are fundamentally problematic and I will show you how we can rethink them entirely. We need to do one of those 180° turns that occur in science and medical reports and reimagine or rethink the very language that we use all the time. To do this, I will get you to think about language use as a virtual reality – indeed, to think of language as the *original virtual reality*.

New metaphors to help rethink how people work

To help you get a gut feel for these weird 180° shifts in thinking about yourself and others, I will present some metaphors. Why have I used metaphors? The answer is that I am not on the whole giving you new evidence or data to consider but I am asking you to make a radical shift in how you talk and think about people and what they do. We are at a stage in understanding people where just adding new evidence will not help, I believe, because the evidence is collected and interpreted in terms of the current thinking, so we are collecting the wrong sorts of evidence with the wrong methods. Similarly, I do not believe we need new, over-arching theories ('grand' theories) that try to explain everything. Generally, these just add more layers to the old ways of thinking or add more components to the same frameworks, so we will not get breakthroughs that way either. We end up with very abstract bio-neuro-psycho-socio-politico frameworks, or large charts of complicated systems diagrams, neither of which have I found helpful.

What is currently needed, I believe, are whole new ways of thinking about people, and I am not going to pretend that I have the best theory with the most evidence. What I want to do is to use new metaphors to trigger you into new ways to 'think people'. Doing this is not something that happens quickly or through logical insight. So I will give metaphors to get you started thinking in new ways, and if at the end of that you get to some understanding different from mine, then that is fine!

One main inspiration for this approach is the philosophy of Deleuze and Guattari (e.g. 1981, 1994). They saw philosophy as an enterprise for presenting new ways of looking at things, issues, and questions until you could *think them* differently – new 'becomings'. They kept raising new metaphors and images to see through traditional problems and blockages in philosophy, art, and science (Deleuze & Guattari, 1994).

Metaphors, therefore, are not new evidence or more clever logical arguments. They are there to teach you that you ***can*** radically rethink how you think at present. It is possible! I am not trying to get you to believe my version of understanding people (at least in this book), but to demonstrate through the book that you can burst out of your thinking ruts and habits and that there are new possibilities or multiplicities. In fact, Deleuze and Guattari (1994) argue that philosophy teaches us new ways to think, art teaches us new ways to look and attend, and science teaches us new ways to affect or interact with the world (Colebrook, 2002).

Psychology and psychiatry have used a number of metaphors since their inception, but most have been taken from the common-sense metaphors we use in everyday life (Leary, 1990; Soyland, 1994). This makes it even more difficult to change your way of thinking about people. For example, probably the hardest shift in the whole book is to think about all those events we label as 'psychological' as existing out in the external world primarily and not going on 'inside our head' when we do things. That is really difficult to do, and most people have trouble because of the long and thorough indoctrination Western society has given us to think that our psychology is 'inside' us. So the metaphors in this book are meant to demonstrate that you *can* think in a different way, even if you are reading a new metaphor and not a logical proof or some newly collected evidence.

I admit these metaphors are difficult to conceptualize in many cases, especially when you tackle them to make sense of your own experiences. It sometimes helps me to think about the many other wrong metaphors that nonetheless seem real to us most of the time – the obviously flat Earth; our soul or psyche being in our heart; or that the Sun and the whole solar system revolve around the Earth. All the metaphors and changes in the thinking of physics were also 'clearly false' when they were first suggested (as Galileo found out). Even now it can be difficult in real-life experience to imagine that the Earth is not flat or that our planet is revolving around the Sun at a high speed (depending on how you measure it).

In fact, much of my inspiration comes from the metaphors used in physics, because physics is considered the most objective and hard-core of all the sciences but has rapidly and wildly changed its metaphors in the last century. At the turn of the twentieth century the study of physics had to undergo many major rethinkings (Gregory, 1988; Gribben, 1984). Some of the shifts in this thinking are comparable to what I want to try here, but not identical. You might also remember that Einstein did not initially produce any new evidence or data or logical arguments – he just changed physicists' ways of thinking about matter and energy. Even now, one of the main metaphor shifts in physics that some resisted (including Einstein, ironically) is that when we try and think about the nucleus of an atom and the quantum details of what is happening, *we should absolutely not try and visualize this*. We need to stop picturing the atom as like, say, a little solar system with electrons orbiting around the nucleus. Enough properties are known that cannot be understood this way and which lead to unnecessary paradoxes. There is nothing like what we call a 'particle' at a subatomic level. Most people cannot even imagine how to think this now, but the metaphor has changed.

This example is extreme but the same radical shifts are urgently needed in psychology and the social sciences, I believe. For example, when we see people do things, or they do things to us, all the metaphors used by academic psychology are based around metaphors that physicists call *particle-thinking* – light particles come off people and bounce into our eyes, which triggers a reaction down the nervous system, etc. I will later urge you, following the 'hard science of physics', to try and change this to *wave-thinking* instead, or a mixture of wave and particle properties as a new metaphor. You will be able to see your world and the people in your world in new ways. You will be able to 'think' them differently.

So when you come across my metaphors in this book, remember that I am mainly trying to get you to have a strong gut feel for them, even if you are not convinced, and then try them out whenever you think about what people do. They are all possible and they all can lead you to new ways of thinking about people and understanding people. If what I am suggesting does not make sense, or you have an 'obvious' objection, try the metaphors out in real life, as this usually clears up some of the misconceptions. For example, if I suggest that human actions are controlled from the outside and not the 'inside', many people just argue or state that that is clearly false (*déjà vu* for Galileo). However, their objections always include assumptions and thinking which I am also trying

Table 1.1 Metaphors that will be presented in this book

Chapter	*Metaphors*
1. Understanding our own psychology	• Our actions are like lumps of Plasticine • Contexts not causes for growing seeds into plants • Contextual observations of holistic elephants
2. The ubiquitous social	• Understanding people is better thought of as attuned responding to external contexts using wave-thinking • We can utilize gravity even if physicists do not understand how it works • Attunement can be thought of as sympathetic resonance
3. Language use as the original virtual reality	• Language use as the original virtual reality • Language better thought of as attuned responses to waves than as reactions to particles • Getting hit 100 percent by a brick and other brute facts of life
4. Thinking, self-talk, and how to read minds	• Thinking can also be reimagined as virtual reality • Thoughts as effects of waves rather than emitted particles
5. The Zen of running our lives	• None. You are safe

to change, so wait a bit and try the metaphor again later. In the present example, once you start to 'get a feel for' the 'ubiquitous social' metaphors, then the metaphor that 'behavior' is brought about from outside of us, not 'inside', makes a lot more sense and you will be able to think it and even 'see' it when you watch people.

To give you some warning in advance, the metaphors I will present are brought together in Table 1.1.

To remind you, these metaphors are intended to spur you to new ways of thinking, not give you all the answers or a grand theory that explains everything. There is no one approach to understanding people that these new metaphors produce; the results of rethinking will be varied and my versions will be different from yours. It is also important to remember that they each help you rethink the others, so try and learn them all, because objections to a single metaphor will be answered by another. How you then might do analyses in real life with real people is a topic covered elsewhere (Guerin, forthcoming).

What will be different after rethinking?

To help you decide whether to read further or not, let me outline how your thinking might be different after reading this book. This will give you a heads-up on new ways you will be able to think about people and what they do. You can think of these as new skills I will teach you – how to see people do things and then be able to think them in a new way.

The first thing is that, on the whole, what has been *observed* about people, and what has been *documented* in a rigorous fashion, will still be the same even after a major rethink. We might rethink whether the current metaphor of cognitive processing best explains why someone laughs at a comedian but we are not in a position to state that the laughing did not happen! Despite any rethinking, the events or phenomena that you have observed will still be there. I am not going to teach you that people do not laugh; just that how we think about people laughing can be done in totally new ways.

On the other hand, there will be many changes to the way you respond when observing people and trying to understand them. The metaphors in this book should lead you to be able do the following:

- To understand people, you will be looking at and recording the vast *contexts* from which their actions emerge, rather than looking for a cause inside their head and blaming people for what their 'mind' does when things go wrong ('cognitive distortions').
- For your better understanding of either groups of people or individuals you will be including contexts of economics, social relationships, cultural or group patterns, historical context, and the contexts of opportunities for those people.
- The contexts for any human actions arising will be primarily to do with *other people* – I will try to get you rethinking that almost all our actions arise in *social* contexts even if we do not commonly talk about them as such and even if the relevant people are not present when the events in question occur.
- You will be better prepared when observing people to see that the contexts from which human actions emerge are frequently hidden or very difficult to observe; and rather than opting for the cheap solution of attributing hypothetical 'inner' causes when you cannot see an obvious external context, you will utilize research and practical methods for finding those hidden external controls.
- We will see later that we can use these contexts as a way of 'reading' people's minds that is realistic with the new metaphors but difficult.
- For anything to do with understanding language and why people say what they say, you will be looking at the social relationships involved,

not the relationships between the person and the 'thing' that they are 'referring to'; we will see that language only does things to people, not to referents.

- When someone says something you will be first thinking about and trying to document *who the audiences were* for those comments – not the meanings of the comments or whether they are true or false, which are the current ways of thinking.
- When you hear someone say something, instead of looking for the meaning of what they have said, you will be looking for the strategic role of those words within some social relationship or social setting.
- For people talking to themselves or referring to 'inner' talk you will be looking for ways that these emerge primarily from external social relationships – not from an inner sanctum of 'private' thoughts. Even for self-talk or thinking you will still need to ask, *who has been or will be the audience for that?*

In all, I believe there are serious and important ways that your behavior towards people will change when you rethink in these ways. You do not need to change your talking for the everyday uses in your life, just when you are working as a professional or you want a better understanding of people.

Why bother?

A good question to ask before you attempt to rethink everything you know about people is whether anything is going to be gained by doing this. I have already suggested that such rethinking, at least in science and medicine, can be fun and astounding; but is there more to be gained than just this? I will answer this question properly right at the end of the book, when I hope the full impact of the changes I and others are suggesting becomes more 'thinkable' to you, but a taste now would be helpful.

For me, the major reason of importance for rethinking how we understand people arises from how we in turn think about helping ourselves and other people, especially those with 'mental health' issues. In the past, most of the treatments and programs to help people through issues and crises have come directly from the way we think about people – mostly rigid theories – and these have usually been found lacking. Psychologists or psychiatrists have some idea (thinking) about how people work and they devise their treatments and solutions based on these. Freud is a good example of someone who did this, as are cognitive-behavioral theories, and the DSM series.

It is my view that at present we have many forms of mental health treatments and programs that can actually work better but which do not fit with the current thinking (Bentall, 2009). Most of these treatments and programs have come directly from practical work with people without relying on standard ways of conceptualizing how people work or theorizing about this. Even if they have helped, however, they have not been given credence because there is no underlying thinking that fits with the current thinking. The practical methods do not fit with any ideas of thinking, so they are ignored.

For example, 'social work' solutions are not seen as appropriate to 'psychological' problems, only because of the way 'psychological' problems are talked about as 'inner' problems and not part of the bigger societal contexts of a person's life. There is also a slew of so-called 'Third Wave' behavior therapies which seem to work well but which I do not think have a great conceptual basis yet. But the changes in thinking which I suggest here will progress that goal by giving new ways to 'think through' practical methods that work but which do not fit current theories. There are also many medicinal or drug therapies that are given in part because they have been seen to have at least some positive effects; but in part they are also given because of some vague thinking that 'inner' brain function and chemicals control 'inner' human actions, so we need to change the brain chemicals to fix people's problems. All these are not completely wrong, but the current ways of thinking about people, which I believe are wrong, are directing how we treat people.

A second reason for rethinking is that it can potentially change the way we interact with each other, think about each other and what we are doing, and allow a better understanding of why people do the things they do. All human relationships have conflicts and problems, but a better way of thinking about these conflicts and problems can be achieved through a major rethinking. I am hopeful of this, at least.

Finally, it should be said that I do not have all the answers for understanding people and what they do. However, new ways of thinking about people will lead us out of some impasses that have blocked our moving forward in understanding people. While I do not have the answers to what exactly will come out of rethinking the metaphors that have held sway for a long time in psychology, I am confident that new and more creative and practical solutions to human issues will be found.

Causes and contexts: shifting metaphors from current psychology

To help you get started on rethinking how you understand what people do, this chapter will look at two very fundamental shifts in thinking that differ from current academic psychology. The *first* is the shift from causes to contexts. The overwhelming thinking about and understanding of people's actions, almost undisputed in academia since Descartes, is that actions originate inside the person in some form or another. This idea has been in partnership with the *second* fundamental idea that I also want you to try and rethink here – that the causes for human action are constructed moment by moment in a sequence and then spring into action.

Starting in the 1960s academic world, the 'cognitive revolution' totally changed the metaphor of thinking about people into one of 'cognitive information processing', comparing people to mini-computers. This was a new 'particle' way of talking which suggested that our brains (and eyes, ears, etc.) take in and process particles of 'information', compute and decide in the brain what to do, and then instruct the body what to do next. This metaphor has become so ingrained in Western culture that it is now bandied around media and academia alike as if it were gospel, and the only metaphor possible. Here is a common form:

sensations → perception → memory → retrieval → cognition → action.

In order to 'understand' humans we need to know all the steps in this 'particle' chain. Currently, there is a big metaphorical focus on the involvement of the brain in the middle steps, with the implicit idea that we cannot understand human actions at all without understanding how the brain 'processes' the particle-information that is whizzing down these chains.

This is just one example of ingrained ways of thinking that are unquestioned in academic psychology except by a few (Bentley, 1935; Gibson, 1979; Guerin, 2001; Powers, 2005; Reed & Jones, 1982). However, many psychologists and others are now beginning to see these forms of cognitive information processing thinking as inhibiting new ways forward in thinking, researching, and helping people.

Let me give an example which should appear innocuous in its commonness. I am walking down a street when my brain or eyes 'notice' a car weaving wildly, coming towards me. My cognitive processing (or ego, or brain processes, or self, or spirit, or reason) computes (or decides, or intuits) that the car will hit me so this inner thinking causes my muscles to get into action and I run off the side of the road to avoid being hit by the car.

Three key things to notice from this example:

- that this deciding or computing takes place 'inside' the person even if it is deemed to be 'automatic';

- that the deciding or computing takes place in real time (or must be fully understood from real-time micro events);
- that the deciding or computing is utilizing a relatively *unchanging inner environment* which deals with new data but is itself unchanged.

These are *three key ideas I want to dispute* and, more importantly, I want to *get you to be able to think otherwise.*

I will admit that after two or more centuries of thinking this way it is difficult to rethink these three ideas, although some writers have tried to convince people otherwise over the centuries. So what I want to do is not to give you logical reasons against these three ideas, or new evidence, but rather to show you some more concrete ways you can begin to rethink these ideas in new ways. So what ideas am I going to push onto you instead? Let me state them boldly here and then I will fill in more details for you to be able to wield them yourself.

- Our experiences and the consequences of our actions *change us* so that we act immediately and do not have to recompute every micro second – meaning that we do not have an unchanging 'processing' environment (this chapter).
- Our words about our actions, how we commonly talk about them, have fooled us into thinking these century-old ideas (this will be in Chapter 3).
- Our talking to ourselves or thinking do not control our actions (Chapter 4).
- The fundamental contexts of all human action are external social contexts, not anything 'inner' (Chapter 2, primarily).
- Talking to self is about responding to people later, not about computing a decision to act (Chapter 4).
- These social contexts are, for various reasons, not obvious to us and in many cases work better if they are hidden.

My teaching experience has been that until people get a gut feel for these points – that we act without having to construct inner pictures or plans – then it is more difficult for them to begin to think and see the social contexts which will replace the 'inner causes' of actions. So I will try to get you rethinking the first of these here and then move on to the ubiquity of social contexts in Chapter 2.

Sequential, causal, or contextual basis for human actions?

The first rethinking I wish to do is that of dispelling the myth that new actions are developed, computed, or decided sequentially in real time in the head. We need to be rid of this in order to allow the external locus of 'the mind' to be revealed, especially the subtle social controls over our actions.

To do this I will use my first metaphor. Embarrassingly, this is an extremely low-tech metaphor. It is especially embarrassing because it is trying to replace the complex, high-tech metaphors of computers and information-processing machines with a new one of hitting a lump of Plasticine! Bear with me.

Metaphor 1. Our actions are like lumps of Plasticine

Let me start with a very simplified example. I am not suggesting that our behavior is controlled by putty or Plasticine, nor that the brain is filled with these substances (although I suspect this with some people). What I want to get across is the pattern of rethinking in a metaphor to replace the sequential, causal thinking we are constrained to use at present.

- Imagine a spherical ball of putty or Plasticine. It behaves in certain ways. If you put it on a slope, for example, it will roll smoothly down, probably in a straight line (if the slope is even). If you spin it, it will probably keep rotating smoothly for a while. If you tip water onto it, the water will all run off.
- Now imagine that you get a hammer and give the Plasticine a couple of minor blows. There are now a couple of serious dents in it. Lo and behold, the behavior has changed also, and immediately. If you put it on a slope it will not run down at all now, or else it will clump its way down in a jiggardly manner. If you spin it, it probably will not spin for long, although it is possible that the damage did not change its spin axis. If you tip water onto it, it is likely to hold some of the water in the dents you made.
- My only point is about how we think about the change in behavior here. We ***would not say*** that after being hit, the (ex)sphere of Plasticine computes its new shape, computes the slope and the forces involved, and then causes the jiggardly rolling motion down the slope. We would not say that it was processing information about the hammer blows and producing and *memorizing* a cognitive representation or model of its new shape and then using that representation or model to decide how it will roll.
- What we ***would say*** is that the devastating hammer blows changed the very substance of the Plasticine sphere so that when we put it on the slope, the (ex)sphere just rolls differently, and does so

immediately. It does not need to think about it or compute or represent anything. It was changed in its very structure by the consequences of the hammer blows so that the new behavior just occurs without any moment-by-moment or sequential planning or deciding or thinking. We do not suppose that there is a storage area somewhere in the Plasticine that remembers the shape and type of dents and that these memories are then used to help calculate all future actions. If we want to talk about a remembering at all, it is that *the actual structural changes in the object* ***are*** *the remembering.*

Can you see the point of this rethinking, even though it is embarrassingly low-tech? Human actions and repeated actions are certainly more complicated than this simplified example, but the thinking involved is what I want you to focus upon. *Instead of thinking in terms of a separate and unchanging part of the object or organism storing and processing a representation of whatever just happened in order to plan the next move, we can think it through in another way: that the organism is directly changed by what happens, and those changes* ***are*** *already part of the context for the next actions without anything else having to be processed or decided or planned in a middle sequence.*

We certainly, as complex humans, get a strong experience that there are often processes going on before we act. For example, if I ask you, "Which color hat do you want?" you experience what seems to be 'processing' of some sort going on, before you act. However, I will deal with these experiences below if you can suspend any challenges based on the feeling that a lot of 'processing' usually goes on before you act. For now I want you to learn a new way of thinking, a new logic for thinking about the production of human actions. Later, in Chapter 4, I will argue, as others have, that any pre-action 'thinking' does not actually control our behavior even though it sure seems that way – almost as certainly as it seems the Earth is flat. That will help you understand this current metaphor with the more complex human behaviors when we get there.

A key point to focus on now though, to help you make a 180° shift in your thinking, is about the 'unchanging processing part' of human actions. We normally have a hidden assumption that, like a conveyor belt in a factory, we have an unchanging processor part that moves 'information' (our particles) along from the senses and does things to that information, and moreover that this processing part is not changed by anything that happens during that process. It is also like a computer chip that does things to the electrons buzzing around it but remains itself unchanged at the end of the day (in fact, there are now smarter chips that do get changed!). Closer to home, it seems obvious in everyday life that it is our ***brains*** that do not change even as they pass information around and change it – our mind or brain stays about the same no matter what 'particles' our senses send through to us.

Instead of the unchanging processing conveyor belt in our brain or mind, I want you to rethink this way: when some event happens to us, we are changed by the consequences in a number of ways that are then the direct or immediate context for acting differently in that context next time, and we then act differently immediately and 100 percent without having to go through any representation, computing, or deciding, because we have been previously changed in some way (in terms of later metaphors, we will call this being 'reattuned' to the 'affordances' of the world). Now, this rethinking is very hard to do, especially when, as I have already said, our experience seems to be that there are representations and images and all sorts of planning and deciding internal events between what happens once and what happens another time. We will deal with pre-action 'thinking' in Chapter 4. Just think of yourself as a spherical ball of Plasticine, if that helps!

I actually find that this metaphor can be quite refreshing in life, like a good Zen or mindfulness moment. Try this: you stop reading, walk outside, and imagine that for the first time, you talk to your neighbor. The way to think now, with the new Plasticine metaphor, is that the next time you go outside to your neighbor's fence, it is like you are a new person (albeit in a minor way)! Both you and that neighbor and your social context are now different. When you talk for the second time you will be different and behave differently immediately. So you can think that *after each and every experience in life you are a new and changed person* – you immediately behave differently, like the Plasticine ball. As mentioned, this metaphor can be refreshing. It shows us that we are constantly reinventing or reshaping ourselves through doing things.

To go back now to the earlier example of a weaving car coming towards you, we could perhaps rethink this way: from all the life events of things coming towards you fast, you have been changed to act in certain ways in those contexts or similar contexts (Gibson, 1979, would call them *affordances*). If you can now ignore for the moment all the verbal chatter going on 'inside your head' when a car comes weaving straight towards you out of control, then what happens is that you act in ways that *you are already shaped to act* because of all your earlier history – you do not need to stand there and compute what to do from a memory storage while the car is accelerating towards you. If you have not been changed previously by experiences of fast things coming at you, then goodbye.

Now one of the problems for this attempt to rethink is that people often do just stand there looking as if they are talking inside their heads while a car is coming towards them, and they might later report a lot of chatter going on. But, to give you a heads-up, we will see in Chapter 4 that they are most likely 'lost in thought' about *how they would talk to others* about this car coming towards them event, or be pre-emptively rehearsing how they will comment to others about the situation – if they survive that is! In fact, military personnel, Third Wave therapists, 'inner game' proponents (Green, 1986), and others teach you to get rid of this chatter and just act from 'instinct', which means acting on the basis of changes that have been made to you from all your earlier experiences or training in context. Zen and Zensunni practitioners have also trained this for centuries. Get rid of the chatter – its usefulness is for something other than acting; its usefulness is social, as we shall see.

Why do we think action is sequential and constantly decided?

I have just presented the first twist in thinking, although I do not expect you to get it immediately. Took me ages! You will need to think of real examples in your own life to work through, and I will present many more as we go through that might help. Also, when some of the other pieces fall into place, as you rethink your life with other metaphors, the whole idea of everything being decided and represented on the spot as we act in life will seem less and less plausible. And when in Chapter 4 you get the new idea that the chatter in your head does not cause your actions in any case, then you might want to come back and reread this.

This leads me to one of the endeavors I believe I have a duty to tackle. If I am going to seriously argue for rethinking our ideas about people at 180° then I have an obligation to discuss why it is that we all go happily about our business thinking 'wrongly', at least according to me and others. How could we all have got it so wrong for so long? This is something popular science writers do not often do. They claim something like "Eating cabbage causes cancer" but then fail to discuss how it is that nobody else ever had an inkling about this.

I have already hinted above that both academics and non-academics go along with the "moment-by-moment-decision-making-causing-our-actions" idea because of their information processing metaphors. The main reason, though, why people do not rethink this idea also applies to almost all the rethought ideas in this book.

It is the same one Einstein presented when introducing his Theory of Relativity, which, although far more important than the ideas in this book, made people totally rethink the universe (Einstein, 1924/2007). This reason is that in ordinary everyday life, it does not make much of a difference whether you rethink or not. Even after Einstein presented his new ideas, the old Newtonian physics was still basically correct and made correct predictions in ordinary dimensions of size at ordinary speeds with ordinary objects. Nothing much was disturbed. You could still make your cup of tea or coffee even if the gravity of your cup was a fold in space-time.

Einstein's Theory of Relativity did make a huge difference, though, in two ways. First, if physicists were dealing with large masses, very fast speeds, or super-small objects (which are no longer even 'objects' in a quantum universe), then the old ways of thinking did not work – the old ways of thinking needed to be changed in those cases. Second, and of more interest to us, even if the Newtonian ideas worked for ordinary sizes and speeds, Einstein's rethinking forced people to rethink a lot of other related concepts and ideas (and equations) that *did* apply to ordinary sizes and speeds and this led to other discoveries and other rethinkings.

So in the same way, rethinking with my first metaphor does not change much in everyday life, and we can get on sufficiently with what we do. We can still believe that when a car is speeding towards us we immediately (on-the-spot) compute what to do next on the basis of retrieving stored memories and computing probable outcomes before acting. However, when there are unusual or extraordinary events, and there are certainly many weird human behaviors and actions, then the rethink becomes necessary. And moreover, the rethink will force us to rethink a lot more, even about ordinary behavior and how we try and change people's actions when appropriate. These other rethinks are set out in this book and they certainly do impact on everyday life. You might want to consider why it is that all those professional trainers I mentioned earlier work hard to stop the chatter in your head and get you to act without thinking or deciding.

As an example of a weird action, I remember being very impressed and puzzled as a boy when reading that Neil Armstrong, who later first stepped on the Moon, had an earlier mission in which his spacecraft went out of control and was spinning around *once a second*. Armstrong did not panic or wait and compute what to do, he calmly proceeded to do the correct actions without wasting time and thinking about it. Likewise we want to understand how Buddhist monks can set themselves alight with petrol in protest, or how prisoners can starve themselves to death.

To understand these things we needed a better or broader way of understanding all that is going on in these contexts, so a new approach is warranted. I will get back to these examples when all the rethinking gets put together in Chapter 5.

Thinking contextually

Having set out some problems for thinking causally when trying to understand people and what they do, I need to say a bit more about thinking contextually. More will come later but the change in thinking needs be started now.

It often seems as if there are a few obvious or salient causes for why people do what they do. When students are late for lectures I absolutely know either that (1) they are lazy or (2) missed the bus. What you must always think, however, when you get tempted to go along with this are these points:

- There are many other 'causes' around, but ones which do not happen to be salient to us.
- Whether something *seems* to be obvious or salient in a situation is a function of: many other events; the way we talk and observe; our histories; what people will agree with if we tell them causes; what people will challenge if we say it out loud.
- There are always many background events (contextual events) that must be working in conjunction with the salient-looking 'causes', and there are no good reasons why they should be left out when understanding why people do what they do (Kantor called these 'setting events' and emphasized their importance for our understanding the total 'field' or context; Kantor & Smith, 1975).

Finally, if you still believe that hard-nosed physicists like to think causally, here is a summary of where 'cause' has gotten to in current quantum physics:

> No longer can we regard the present as the final consequence of a single, unbreakable chain of events. Instead, we must consider all the 'undismissed possible pasts' that *might* have contributed to the present. Causation ceases to be *particular* and becomes somewhat *holistic*. Since it is the nature of waves that each part of the wave can influence the future of all other parts of a wave, it is in this sense that a particle is 'wave-like'.
>
> (March, 1992, p. 233)

For the astute reader, the connection between 'holistic' and 'contextual' will be obvious, and will continue through the next chapters. Especially when we get to our holistic elephants!

Metaphor 2. Contexts not causes for growing seeds into plants

Let me give another example of moving from cause to context, not to logically persuade you but to get you thinking a bit differently. When we plant a seed and watch it grow later on, it does not usually occur to us to talk about *the cause* of the seed's growth. We usually talk instead about the 'conditions' necessary for good growth. It seems pointless to single out one element and say, for example, that "sunlight is the cause of plants growing". If we have a lot of sun but poor soil then the seed will not grow.

Let me make two more points about the seed example to elaborate on the points given earlier. First, we do not attribute an internal cause and say that the seed initiated and maintained the process of growth because it wanted to, or was motivated. Instead, we look at the external conditions (context) while also noting the makeup of the 'internal' seed environment. Second, the seed example above is artificially biased towards one single outcome – good growth. In fact, all conditions have effects on the seed but only some combinations lead to *good growth*. What we should say instead, to be accurate, is that *any and all conditions affect the plant 100 percent* but that only some lead to the outcome in which we are interested (in many conditions, for example, the seed *rots* 100 percent). So instead of:

Cause X → SEED → Growth

We would rethink as:

Put Context X around SEED and you will get Growth 1 (growing)

Put Context Y around SEED and you will get Growth 2 (rotting)

Put Context Z around SEED and you will get …

The final things to notice about this example (but which are relevant to our human examples) are these:

- Many factors in the seed context are *hidden or not salient* so we do not easily observe them (such as nitrogen deficiency) and so they get used less by us as the purported causes only because they are invisible or difficult to see.
- Many factors in the context are *complex* so we do not easily observe them as salient causes (previous legume crops in the same

field affect our seeds in future years) and find it difficult to report them (and hence we leave them out).

- Both the above points are to do with social responding, not the world of the seed.

So often it 'looks' as if a single cause has occurred leading to a response of growth or rotting, but this is very misleading.

Now the same rethinking needs to occur for thinking about people, although I am quite aware that the contexts and outcomes are much more complex than for seed growth. But you can see the same patterns, since causal thinking has led to both of these in the history of psychology:

Stimulus X → Brain or black box → Response

Stimulus X → real-time information extraction and cognitive processing → Response

Instead, your thinking needs to be:

- Wrap Context X around a Person and you will get Action 1
- Wrap Context Y around a Person and you will get Action 2.

It must again be emphasized that this is not easy to rethink and the contexts will be very complex and very difficult to observe for people. Rethinking does not mean the answers are immediately given or are easy. The consequences of all our past contexts and history are part of our current context (like the Plasticine metaphor), as is clear when we put Person 1 into Context X and they do one thing, but put Person 2 into Context X and they do something different. This at least allows for the diversity and variations we find in human behavior rather than assume the same cause will always bring about the same outcome for everyone, as contemporary metaphors often imply. But it does make our observations and interventions more difficult, although I will present a metaphor below to help improve you skills in 'contextual observation'!

We do not have a 'control center'

What has been given so far also leads to another 180° shift in thinking: that we need to stop thinking about there being a 'control center' inside each of us that primarily directs all actions and thought. We certainly have a strong sense or feeling that a 'we' or 'I' controls our actions, so there must be something behind this (just like the flat Earth). I argue that we think this way partly because, in the absence of seeing what externally controls our actions, we have a long intellectual and common-sense tradition of attributing effects to an 'inner cause' as a cheap substitute. Where you cannot observe what is controlling your actions outside of you (perhaps something from your history, in fact), then that is where there will be a preponderance of causal attributions to 'inner control'. These inner controls have gone by all sorts of names in the past – self, ego, executive control, information processing, me. I even argue that psychology as a discipline can be defined by its being a historical dumping ground, as it were, for human actions and activities for which the external controls are not easily seen and which are thus deemed 'psychological' issues.

Another reason we tend to think that there are 'inner' causes for what we do is because we really do have a sense of controlling our own actions – I 'know' that I wanted to do X and then I went and did it. However, I will later argue that this is also flawed and once we rethink the roles and functions of language use, then we can properly rethink this feeling of control. I will argue in Chapter 4 that the 'feeling' comes from the 'talking as if to ourselves' which we do while acting *but that the talking as if to ourselves does not actually control what we are doing*. The talking-as-if-to-ourselves is only there to prepare for what other people might do or say to us after the actions. But these self-dialogues indisputably do give us the impression of controlling our actions! Just as the Earth really does seem flat when I am in the deserts of Central Australia.

A final reason (for now; there is more in Chapter 4) as to why we normally think in terms of an inner control for what we do is related to a further 180° rethink. We are accustomed to think in terms of one event 'causing' another, like one billiard ball hitting another and causing the second one to move. But it was argued above that this is a poor metaphor for thinking about people's actions. Like with ecological thinking, we must get away from thinking in terms of causes and effects and move to thinking in terms of *contexts* which bring about, ferment, or assemble what occurs. That argument has been given above, but the new point here is that when we think in terms of causes then we are more prone to think about our own actions as being 'caused' by an 'inner' form of control. The causal thinking is misdirecting us about what gets us to do the things we do. And I hope that rethinking the use of causal thinking will help you also rethink the use of 'inner causes' for explaining why you do what you do.

Contextual observation

It should be clear from the above that what we observe and document will change when we have begun to rethink contextually. We cannot just perform superficial (including repeated cross-sectional) measurements or observations and then attribute causes to hypothetical 'inner' causes or the most salient cause we were able to observe. The message is *that we must always assume there are important parts of the context for any human actions that are not salient, and ones that cannot be reported by people verbally, but which need careful observation and documentation.*

I will address this more in the course of the book, but to get you started, and to help you not just *think* contextually but also *observe* contextually, I will briefly present how Arthur F. Bentley wrote about the activity of observation. This should guide you into rethinking your own observations.

Bentley was one of many great thinkers (or rethinkers?) who did not become famous because their way of thinking did not fit with the contemporary metaphors. Bentley (1935) made five points about observation that are relevant here but which you will need time to wrap your head around:

- observation is done over time
- observation is not done by individuals but built up by many people
- observation is not about the eye alone but uses the body and tools
- observation is not an 'innate power' or a given but requires training
- observation works within a bigger construction of 'scientific observability'.

> That which we are accustomed to observing is not all that we can observe. That which we call 'seeing' in the most limited, direct rendering of the word is not all the 'seeing' that we do, it is not even a fair expression for the general situations of our seeing. What we may observe is connected with our need for observation, and is conditioned by frames of observability that we possess in fixated or expanding forms.
>
> (Bentley, 1935, pp. 203–204)

What Bentley is getting at is that common usage of the verb 'to see' is only related to phrases such as "I see a bird." These are cross-sectional uses and not longitudinal or durational uses. He wanted instead to include other phrases such as "I see a bird in flight." Notice the difference? The second phrase is spread over duration and space, and there is no single 'thing' or 'particle' looked at, and so it becomes *contextual* to examine. He goes on to comment that we should also use 'see' to mean any sort of seeing. When I say "I see a bird," should I include the circulation system, cells, feathers, breathing, etc.? If we can use 'see' in the sense of "I see a bird in flight," then we should allow seeing of the whole bird. What does "I see a bird" mean anyway? I see the wings, the feet, the plumage, the beak? We never see a whole bird when we make such a comment and, more importantly, we do not even know (cannot verbally report) what bits we did see. In fact, I suggest that for "I see a bird" *the whole phrase is functionally about giving a name to a listener* (Chapter 4) and not a universal, independent observational report of eternal verities (Guerin, 1990). The whole activity of *talking* about 'seeing' a bird is about influencing a listener or future listener, not about a spontaneous commentary on what is happening in our lives – it is a social event not an observational event.

This was echoed in a different way by Deleuze:

> I have, it's true, spent a lot of time writing about this notion of event: you see, I don't believe in things. *The Fold* returns to this question from another viewpoint. My favorite sentence in the book is "There's a concert tonight." In Leibniz, in Whitehead, there are only events. What Leibniz calls a predicate is nothing to do with an attribute, but an event, 'Crossing the Rubicon'. So they have completely recast the notion of a subject: what becomes of the subject, if the predicates are events?
>
> (Deleuze, 1995, p. 160)

Similarly to the concert tonight, Deleuze would have liked the observational sentence "I see a bird in flight" rather than "I see a bird." And notice that his final question is about questioning the idea of a control center in people, running things for us, as we saw earlier.

My goal is that by the end of this book, if you see someone do something, you will be able to 'see them contextually' – that is, see the economic, social relationship, cultural, historical, etc. contexts. You will not see them briefly and you will not only 'see' what you need to report to others or only what you can easily name. The moral for now is *that you can learn to actually see more.*

Metaphor 3. Contextual observations of (blue) holistic elephants

Bentley also tried to show this contextual usage of 'see' or 'observe' by considering the old story of three wise men sent to observe an elephant but who were blindfolded. Do you know the story? They all had to feel just one part of the elephant and they came back with very different accounts of what they saw. The moral is *usually* meant to be that seeing and observation are inherently biased and that we all have different perceptions even of the same object. Ergo, there is no true reality!

Now Bentley does not deny that they came back with different accounts of an 'elephant'. His point was that this is a fairly useless model of 'seeing' or 'observing'. The 'wise men' are blindfolded, they have limited time, they only get to feel one segment of the elephant, and they do not go all the way around the elephant even. So, yes, if that is what you do to make your observations then you will indeed get varied and 'biased' accounts of observation. But that is a poor way to do things. That is bad science!

It would have been better observation if the wise men in our metaphor had:

- taken off their blindfolds
- spent a lot more time interacting with the elephant and its parts
- explored more of the elephant
- observed the elephant over time when it moved or changed
- shared their observations while making them.

If you do observations in that way – contextually – then everyone will get very similar reports. This is the same as the earlier point that "I see a bird" is very different from "I see a bird in flight." The other moral is that *you should not trust observational reports that are limited by time or movement and are not contextual observations.* And just repeating these short-term observations (sending in the blind men again!) will come up with the same wrong answers again and again. The observations might be reliable but they are still false.

The rethinking to take away from Chapter 1

To finish Chapter 1, I will summarize all the bits of rethinking covered so far, keeping in mind that the main discussions for some of these will be made in later chapters after we have covered some new metaphors.

No control center or inner control of human actions. Stop thinking about there being a 'control center' inside each of us that primarily directs all actions and thought. There are no internal 'things' as entities, concepts, or explanations, even though there are reasons why we commonly (but mistakenly) think there are.

Not real-time sequential. Human action is not constructed moment by moment in a sequence before springing into action. When an event happens to us, we are changed in a number of ways that are then the new context for acting differently in that context next time, and when that happens we then act differently, *immediately, and 100 percent* without having to go through any representation, computing, or deciding, because we have previously been changed in some way. How we *talk about* these things to ourselves or to others might take longer, but not the actions.

Changed organism. Instead of thinking in terms of a separate and unchanging part of the object or organism storing and processing a representation of whatever just happened in order to plan the next move, we can think it through in another way: that the organism is constantly changed by what happens, and *those changes are part of the context* for the next actions without anything else having to be processed or decided or planned in the middle. Our experiences and the consequences of our actions *change us* so that we act immediately in future and do not have to recompute every micro second. We do verbally chatter a lot about what is happening but that is a separate and social process (Chapters 2 and 4).

Context not cause. We must get away from thinking in terms of causes and effects and move to thinking in terms of *contexts* or arrangements which precipitate what occurs. When we think in terms of causes we are also more prone to think about our own actions as being 'caused' by an 'inner' form of control.

Contextual thinking. Think of there being (complex) contexts in which actions arise every time (100 percent) and these contexts change and remember for us. The external contexts *are* our memory and are *out there* rather than *in here* – so that in a precise context, a precise action occurs. There is never a single cause for any event and looking for and attributing causes is highly selective and biased.

Contextual observation. Contextual control is external to the person and is usually difficult to observe, partly because of the subtleties and the historical changes, and partly because our skills of observation and reporting to others are biased towards seeing 'causes', and only the most salient and nameable ones, and not contexts. Psychology as a discipline can be defined by its being a historical dumping ground for trying to explain abstractly those actions and activities for which the external controls are not easily seen.

With enough detail, the context gives us 100 percent certainty. This point has arisen a few times but I will leave it until Chapter 3 for more. Stay attuned.

There are reasons we do not rethink these ideas in everyday life. In ordinary life, it does not make too much difference if you rethink or not – the old ways of thinking are harmless enough except in special circumstances (such as understanding mental health). We tend to think that there are 'inner' causes for what we do because we have a real sense of controlling our own actions. However, that 'feeling' comes from the talking to ourselves that we do while acting, but the talking to ourselves does not actually control what we do (Chapter 4).

Social contexts govern most human actions. We have touched upon the idea that social contexts are always involved in understanding people (covered in Chapter 2), even for 'mind', 'mental', and 'cognition' (Chapter 4). The social contexts for various reasons are not obvious to us and in fact work better if they are hidden, so we invent 'inner' causes and many metaphors of the 'inner'. I have heard the construction of metaphorical inner worlds being called psychology's version of 'interior decoration'.

Language use is always in a social context. I have also hinted that we do not use language to express things or ideas, to communicate ideas, to refer to things, or to represent things and ideas. Language use always involves audiences, whether present or not (more in Chapter 3).

References

Barrow, J. D. (2007). *New theories of everything: The quest for the ultimate explanation*. Oxford: Oxford University Press.

Bentall, R. P. (2009). *Doctoring the mind: Why psychiatric treatments fail*. London: Penguin Books.

Bentley, A. F. (1935). *Behavior knowledge fact*. Bloomington, IN: Principia Press.

Chown, M. (2007). *Quantum theory cannot hurt you: A guide to the universe*. London: Faber and Faber.

Colebrook, C. (2002). *Gilles Deleuze*. London: Routledge.

Deleuze, G. (1995). *Negotiations, 1972–1990*. New York: Columbia University Press.

Deleuze, G., & Guattari, F. (1981). Rhizome. *I&C*, 8, 49–71.

Deleuze, G., & Guattari, F. (1994) *What is philosophy?* London: Verso.

Deloria, V. (1999). *Spirit and reason: The Vine Deloria reader*. Golden, CO: Fulcrum Publishing.

Einstein, A. (1924/2007). *Relativity: The special and general theory*. East Bridgewater, MA: Signature Press.

Gibson, J. J. (1979). *The ecological approach to visual perception*. Boston: Houghton Mifflin.

Green, B. (1986). *The inner game of music*. London: Pan Books.

Gregory, B. (1988). *Inventing reality: Physics as language*. New York: John Wiley.

Gribbin, J. (1984). *In search of Schrödinger's cat: Quantum physics and reality*. London: Bantam Books.

Guerin, B. (1990). Gibson, Skinner, and perceptual responses. *Behavior and Philosophy*, 18, 43–54.

Guerin, B. (2001). Replacing catharsis and uncertainty reduction theories with descriptions of the historical and social context. *Review of General Psychology*, 5, 44–61.

Guerin, B. (forthcoming). *Understanding people through social contextual analysis: A practical guide*. Abingdon: Routledge.

Hawking, S. W. (1988). *A brief history of time: From the big bang to black holes*. London: Bantam Books.

Kantor, J. R., & Smith, N. W. (1975). *The science of psychology: An interbehavioral survey*. Chicago: Principia Press.

Leary, D. E. (1990). *Metaphors in the history of psychology*. Cambridge, UK: Cambridge University Press.

March, R. H. (1992). *Physics for poets*. London: McGraw-Hill.

Matthews, R. (2005). *25 big ideas: The science that's changing our world*. Oxford: Oneworld Publications.

Penrose, R. (2010). *Cycles of time: An extraordinary new view of the universe*. London: Vintage Books.

Powers, W. T. (2005). *Behavior: The control of perception*. New Canaan, CT: Benchmark Publications.

Reed, E. S., & Jones, R. (Eds.). (1982). *Reasons for realism: Selected essays of James J. Gibson*. Hillsdale, NJ: Lawrence Erlbaum.

Soyland, A. J. (1994). *Psychology as metaphor*. London: Sage.

2 The ubiquitous social

From social constructionism to social contextualism

In analyzing the psychologies in Part I, we witnessed the frequent intrusion of this 'social', and the disturbances it produced for psychological observation and construction. At one extreme we found efforts to exclude it altogether from attention, and at the other, indications that it might inundate the entire territory; elsewhere it was tacitly accepted or unwillingly tolerated. Whatever its treatment, as fact or aspect of fact it was never absent from the psychological problem.

(Bentley, 1935, pp. 187–188)

Psychology and sociology are alike in that their investigations deal with situations in which organisms and environmental objects are involved together in durational events. The systems of such events provide the subjects-matters for both these sciences. Neither psychology nor sociology is ever able to concentrate its exclusive attention upon the organism taken in isolation, nor upon the environmental object so taken.

(Bentley, 1935, p. 283)

In summary, I have never found a situation of behaviors in which I could assume a substantive separation between psychological behavioral facts taken as 'individual' and other behavioral facts taken as 'social', in such a way that I could regard it as reliable for the more general purposes of the organization of behavioral knowledge and the pursuit of behavioral research. I have never found social things in basic separations from individually psychological things, nor individually psychological things in basic separation from social things.

Such being the case, I cannot establish a coherent distinction between the functional techniques of psychology and sociology upon the basis furnished by any rough-and-ready distinction set

> forth or purporting to be guaranteed by the dubious words 'individual' and 'social', or by any of their substitutes.
>
> (Bentley, 1935, p. 329)

The rethinking in this chapter is very subtle but vitally important. Many of the loose ends in other rethinkings only make sense when put into their social context, which is like a 'thinkable glue' that holds them together. Indeed, many thinkers have come unstuck at this point (Dennett, 1969; Nietzsche, 1967). Wittgenstein (1958), for example, went through many arguments against 'private languages' and 'inner thoughts' (covered here in Chapter 4) but could never find a way to reconcile what might really be going on, because he did not see the essential social foundation (hence external context) for all uses of language and thinking – he was still stuck in an individual agency way of thinking.

The 180° rethinking of this chapter is that *all human actions have social relationships at the hub of the contexts or environmental arrangements that bring them about* – even though they sure seem private and individual. Moreover, this arises because *all the resources and things we want come via social contexts*. These social contexts are often hidden and difficult to trace, many are buried in the historical social context, and we will see later that social interactions and relationships usually work better if we do not notice their explicit social control. And as discussed in Chapter 1, there is in addition a long and powerful Western tradition of assuming an 'inner' person to be the cause or controller of human behaviors, especially when there are no obvious or salient external causes jumping out at us. But the argument now is that it is precisely because we cannot see the subtle social contexts for our actions that people instead invent substitute 'inner causes'.

This all gives the reader a hint as to why this rethink is so important, even though I will not make this point explicit until the very end of this chapter – because most of the seemingly weird, unexpected, difficult-to-account-for human actions are those with hidden social contexts bringing them about, but these are the actions typically and culturally 'explained' in terms of inner events, mental illnesses, personality quirks, spirits, etc. If we cannot learn to recognize and indeed anticipate these external but hidden social contexts then we will never understand the weirder behaviors or even the normal ones.

There will be three main ways I want to guide the reader through this difficult reconceptualization:

- through the use of certain metaphors;
- by showing with examples that even when we are alone, we are still in a social situation or context;

- by showing with examples that our 'private' inner thinking and thoughts are also social events and not actually private (Chapter 4).

These are tricky rethinkings but many writers before me have gone along this path in some way and I am drawing on their good work even when I forgo all the referencing (Bentley, 1935; Berger & Luckmann, 1967; Billig, 2011; Burke, Joseph, Pasick, & Barker, 2010; Gee, 1992; Holland, 1977; Newman & Holzman, 1996; Searle, 1995; Simmel, 1950, 1907/1978; Smail, 2005; Wertsch, 1991, 1985). Many of these thinkers emphasize the social but without showing how it links to all behavior, something I will attempt to do for general behavior in this chapter, language use in the next, and thinking and consciousness in the one after that.

The third bullet point above will mainly be covered in Chapter 4, after discussing the generic social context of language use and then extending this to talking or rehearsing talk to oneself (or thinking, as we call it). In this present chapter, I wish to concentrate more on how we can conceive or reimagine that being alone is social and being 'private' is social, so you can learn to be sensitive to the social contexts even for those everyday behaviors that look totally non-social and as if arising from individual or 'inner' agency.

In general, when observing any human behavior I now like to ask these sorts of questions first:

- Who is the audience for that?
- Who were the people or social groups instrumental in bringing that about?
- Who has a stake in this?
- Who is this about?
- Which different audiences are contexts for any conflicting effects here?

To go back to the earlier example of jumping out of the way of a car, the jumping part might not be part of a social context, but the chatter and thinking going on about it certainly is, and notice that this is what will kill you if it takes up too much time: sadly, and ironically, we die rehearsing the way we will talk to people about what is about to happen.

Contextual influence better thought of as waves than particles: three metaphors

I want to begin a difficult new metaphor to help you rethink that we are influenced by our external contexts and not an inner control center, and I will continue this metaphor through the next few chapters. I have already hinted at this in Chapter 1. So this is an important metaphor and I will try and develop it carefully. It will require a bit of flexible thinking from you as well.

The changes in thinking from Chapter 1 are difficult, given the centuries of thinking in the ways we do. But in the struggles I had with this, I was reminded of the changes in thinking that beset physicists at the turn of the last century, when they had to stop thinking with a *particle* physics metaphor and think instead with a *wave* physics metaphor. What happens on top of the sea with your surfboard is better explained using wave ideas than particle ideas. But physicists were using only particle ideas when thinking about what goes on in the smallest unit (at that time) – the atom. They needed to incorporate a lot of wave thinking to get practical answers.

Eventually it dawned on me that there are very similar, but only metaphorically similar, changes in thinking required in psychology and thinking in general about people. But please remember that this is a metaphor – I am not suggesting that this is about the physics of people, or that people communicate or influence each other through mysterious 'psychic' waves. Rather, the point is that instead of being constrained in our ideas by all explanations needing a causal particle to pass energy on to the next one by bumping into it, the use of wave ideas obviates this need. You can actually think differently with waves and this can rescue us from the most common pattern in psychology: that to explain anything properly, we need to describe the path of particles as they move from hitting the retina, through the brain and nervous system, and into motor neurons and then action. I will first present a little background on particles and waves in physics, if you can bear with me. There will be no mathematics.

The whole process of electromagnetic waves is puzzling in real life if you bother to think about it (http://www.youtube.com/watch?v=4e8HT3GGw6c). How does light travel, and *what is light, anyway*? The view from Newton's time and earlier, and probably in most people's lives when they think about it, is that light must be made up of particles that move in a straight line and cause effects on whatever they hit, including the retina of the eye. Indeed, Newton's Laws predicted some of the properties of light quite well – the straight reflections in a mirror, light moving in straight lines rather than curvy ones.

I will not go into details, but some physics experiments and observations started to suggest that the metaphor of particles could not explain everything about the properties of light. You can set up experiments (or read about them – check out the Internet) in which light behaves unlike what we would expect from a bunch of particles moving very fast in a straight line. In the late nineteenth century and early twentieth century, physicists therefore had to have a major rethink, and by changing some preconceived ideas they rethought many physical phenomena. They have not got all the answers yet, but that will also be part of my point (with my later 'gravity metaphor'). I am merely utilizing here the physicists' major change: from thinking in terms of particles and causes to thinking in terms of waves and context.

Here are some quotations showing how the thinking can change:

> When an object acts on other objects without touching them, we say it is surrounded by a field.
>
> (Kowalski & Hellman, 1978, p. 386)

> The basic fact of gravitation is that two masses exert forces on one another. We can think of this as a direct interaction of the two mass particles, if we wish. This point of view is called *action-at-a-distance*, the particles interacting even though they are not in contact. Another point of view is the *field* concept which regards the mass particle as modifying the space around it in some way and setting up a *gravitational field.* This field then acts on any mass particle in it, exerting the force of gravitational attraction on it. The field, therefore, plays an intermediate role in our thinking about the forces between mass particles.
>
> (Halliday & Resnick, 1966, p. 404)

In the case of light, it became clear that there were properties of light that *resembled waves rather than particles*. Some physicists started to treat light as a wave that travels. Let us think now about waves. This is fascinating stuff and you can look at great accounts on the Internet or in books. I am constantly astounded at how waves work in the way that they do. You will need to get a good feel for the following, so try imagining all these waves or go out and observe them.

Let us start with waves in water, ones with which we are familiar. We know that if we drop a stone in a lake, waves are produced and they ripple outwards in all directions, unless constrained by barriers. What is fascinating to me is that waves 'travel' through the water even though the particles of the water do not travel. It is not that some bits of water hit by your stone move outwards and reach the shore. Rather *the 'wave form' travels through the water and any particular bit of water remains exactly where it was after the wave has gone through*. It is amazing to think about this, and this is the sort of change in properties that allows us to rethink a phenomenon. So the wave is not the water – it is something else very real but hard to describe, just like many phenomena we need in order to understand people. That is what got me thinking.

If you look online for some illustrations of waves, here are some things you will find out. First, as I have said, the medium of the waves (in water) does not move, just the wave or the energy or the pattern or whatever you want to call it. Second, when two waves 'hit', unlike particles, *the colliding waves move through one another*. At the point of collision they add up all the 'energy' as it were and become larger, but they then go back to what they were and keep moving. They move independently through one another (except for some minor effects of friction and things). You can check all this out at a lake if you want, or consider that when two people are using mobile phones in the same room they do not interfere with each other.

One of the most important points for physicists trying to understand the properties when considering light as waves, but not of so much interest to us using it as a metaphor, is that for a wave which reaches a small gap in a wall or something, when it gets through on the other side it spreads out. So imagine that your lake has a wall across it and there is a small gap at one place in the wall. Your stone-induced-ripple-wave will travel out in all directions but when it reaches the wall most of it will bounce back again, but where there is the gap some will pass through (the wave, not the water) and then spread right out again in new circles. Now, the point is that particles will never do this. Shoot a particle through the gap and it will continue in a straight line as Newton's Laws would predict, just as a radio-controlled little boat going through that gap will just continue in a straight line – the gap does not cause it to change paths, or spread out as a wave does. Of course if it hits the edge of the gap it will deviate from its straight path.

What this means is that when we think of waves, we have to think with different properties of behavior than when we have particles. The particular 'spreading through a gap' property of waves given above, for example, was important for physicists, because when they did a series of famous experiments in which they shone beams of light through small slits, they found that on the other side the beams produced a spread-out, wave-like pattern. If light was made up simply of little particles the beams should have gone through the slit and made a pin-point on the other side. But what happened was just like the spread of your water waves through the gap in the lake wall.

Now the properties of electromagnetic waves are not quite the same as those of water. For starters, one big difference is that light does not even require a medium. When you drop your stone in the lake the waves require the water to 'carry' it across the lake, even if every little particle of water stays where it was after the wave has traveled through. In the same way, sounds we hear travel outward as waves with air as their medium (in space you cannot hear anyone scream, remember). But light, on the other hand, can travel through space, which is a vacuum containing no matter, unlike the water in the lake (although some physicists tried rethinking that there might be a hypothetical medium, sometimes called ether or aether, that was in space and 'carried' light but that we could not see).

Another property of light that was the same as any other wave was that when light 'collided' with other light they passed through each other. Shine two torches at 90° and their beams do not crash and scatter where they meet but pass straight through (unlike two billiard balls colliding). Light does get reflected back when it hits a mirror (but not a wall so much), but then again water waves bounce back when they hit a wall also.

So at the start of the twentieth century physicists had some real puzzles and needed a big change in thinking (e.g. March, 1992; McEvoy & Zarate, 1999; Serway, Vuille, & Faughn, 2009). Their main problem, as it turned out, was that light seemed to behave sometimes as a bunch of particles (Einstein called them *photons*), and sometimes as waves. Eventually it was realized that there was a range of waves, called electromagnetic waves, of which what we call light is just one small portion that we can see with our eyes. There are infra-red electromagnetic waves and all sorts of other frequencies. They also include the microwaves that we use to cook food, and the waves that are used in television, radio, and mobile phone transmission. We will come back to this last one shortly, in another metaphor.

The final point I wish to make is that this change in thinking for physicists also meant a change away from causal thinking, of particles moving and colliding, to a *contextual* view of what is going on at fast speeds and subatomic sizes. This reflects some of the points and metaphors from Chapter 1.

To summarize this brief and slightly random sketch of a fascinating topic, what are of most interest to help change our thinking are these points:

- Electromagnetic waves are one form of wave that does not require a medium (such as water) in order to propagate and have effects and consequences.
- We do not see the electromagnetic waves happening all around us constantly except the bits our eyes can see, which we call light, but this is highly selective.

- When waves hit each other, in general they do not interfere – they do not compete or collide.
- When waves pass through one another they simply cause a momentary additive form of wave and then the two continue in the same direction they were going in before.
- The waves act independently on the whole.
- There can be multiple waves all around us and acting independently.
- This requires us to stop thinking of light in terms of both particles colliding and causal chains.
- We can discuss and experiment with light without having to give details of a causal chain of particles.

As mentioned several times above, the point of this is not to get you believing that people influence each other, and contexts influence us, through some sort of actual electromagnetic or gravitational field surrounding and influencing people; I want this just to be a metaphor of thinking, based on how physicists changed their whole way of thinking from a particle view to a more contextual view that can still include particles. I just want to get across another way of thinking, not invent a new SciFi world.

I prefer to use the term 'context' for this rather than field – that we are immersed in contexts that arrange or determine what we do but not in a causal, particle-like way. As we saw above in quotations from the work of physicists, some physicists tried to make this change by talking about fields rather than particles, and this has included some psychologists when talking about people. Some have tried the term 'field', and also 'life-spaces' and 'domains', but I think these can give the wrong idea (Kantor & Smith, 1975; Lewin, 1951). For example, the main proponent of a field theory, Kurt Lewin, also included 'inner states' such as language and thinking as (inner) parts of the field rather than treating language use as being in an external field or context, as will be outlined in Chapters 3 and 4.

The point in summary is that if we apply the change of thinking from cause-and-effect particle interactions to contextual events which influence us all with multiple and concurrent wave-like properties, then this allows us to think about people in unique new ways we could not think before.

The main change in thinking for this chapter is about *how we can think that social contexts are everywhere affecting and influencing us without having to specify causal chains, without them being obvious or even easily observed*, and without having to have additive properties of each influence – many such influences can act independently at the same time with the same person without conflict or billiard balls smashing.

Metaphor 4. Understanding people is better thought of as attuned responding to external contexts using wave-thinking

This metaphor requires you to think about how some properties of waves work and to consider that it is possible to think this way without knowing all the details. You are going to star in this metaphor as a receiving/transmission tower that 'picks up' waves from mobile phones, except of course in your real case you are an active, moving tower, not stuck on a hill.

So, imagine, not unrealistically nowadays, that there is a bus with 50 people riding on it and every one of those people is using their mobile phone. In terms of electromagnetic waves, each of those phones is sending out a unique wave signal that travels in all directions for some kilometers. These signals have been found to have wave-like properties on the whole, but we do not need to know all the details of how they travel and how far.

Imagine now that you are a receiving/transmission tower nearby (built for mobile phones and the like, not for sensing X-rays, television, or other electromagnetic wave frequencies). All those different waves will be going through you, the tower, which 'deals with' or responds to those multiple waves happening at the same time. To do this you, the tower, are tuned or ***attuned*** to respond to certain waves because of the way you are built and because of how you have been changed by receiving and transmitting in the past (like our Plasticine metaphor, remember), even if there are 50 waves. I will give you a new metaphor for thinking about the 'attunement' bit next, but for now, this is what life is like for receiving/transmission towers sitting in high places.

To summarize and hopefully clarify so far: you are a receiving/transmission tower having 50 waves pass through you but they do not conflict and collide with each other. For those waves that are attuned to your equipment (if they have a valid phone account), you respond in some way or do something (usually send the wave on to somewhere else depending on the forwarding address encoded in the wave). Your attunement depends on how you are built, how past waves have changed you, or how the IT people have calibrated you.

Now we can apply this metaphor to your real self (as a person, not a tower), and the attunements to your various contexts. I want you to imagine as follows: you are seated reading this book but all around you are contexts that influence you. Metaphorically these are just like the plethora of electromagnetic waves that are buzzing all around you right now – like your neighbor's mobile phone or the television transmissions happening from a transmitting tower somewhere, probably within a few hundred kilometers of where you are at this moment.

Now, the real contexts in which you are immersed (like waves around you) as you are reading are not electromagnetic waves, but are the influences from people you have had experiences with who are now sitting in many locations. I want you to think about them, however, as if they were affecting you like the mobile phone waves above. In doing this there is no longer any need to worry about causal or particle pathways from senses to brain or anything. No need to look for a single 'proximate' stimulus.

Some contexts are in the room influencing you (a poster falls off the wall) while others are spatially and historically not present (your brother has been bugging you, the tree outside has a branch that you need to chop down soon, your bank balance is not looking very healthy, etc.). I do not mean that you are thinking all these things, although there might be some form of murky background of thoughts said to yourself occasionally as you read, or thoughts sort of lurking there being rehearsed so they can be said out loud if someone asks (Chapter 4 will have more about your 'thinklings', as I call them, in this situation). But they are having this wave-like influence upon you nonetheless, just like the receiving/transmission tower.

Of all the contexts which are influencing you at this time, having a reverberating impact on you, only a few are present in what we would normally think of as sensory form – like the poster falling down. Of interest for this chapter is that almost all of these contexts will be an influence that involves other people, even if indirectly. So the tree branch possibly falling down is more an issue of borrowing a chainsaw from your friend than about the tree itself, or an issue of what your partner will say if you do not get it done soon before it falls on their car. As we will see in Chapter 4, which of these become 'thoughts' and which 'thoughts' get rehearsed or edited to potentially say to other people is also primarily an external social matter.

So you are attuned like the transmitter tower to respond to certain waves because of how you are built and your history, and the points here are that: (1) most of these are not present in the room; (2) most are about your social contexts; (3) they are influencing you even if you do nothing overt; (4) they are influencing you even if you do not notice or 'think' them; and (5) they are having a real influence on you, however.

So as you sit where you are now reading this book, the contexts that make up your world are exerting wave pressures on you, meaning they are acting independently, without conflict, without necessarily doing the same thing, and without you noticing them, except perhaps for a couple. We could find out many of these if I were to ask you to tell me all the possible things that you might have been thinking about or considering in any way at this time – what social pressures and issues are upon you now, good and bad? But it would be a waste of time, from a wave-thinking point of view, to try and fill in all the particle causal paths of these influences on your current person. It is better to focus on describing these contexts, asking about their social origins ("who is involved?"), and describing in what ways, if any, you do something different afterwards.

As a good learning experience, try and say or write down all the many 'thoughts' that have been lurking in the background as you read this book. Can you do this? In Chapter 4 we will see some methods used by Freud and others to do this more systematically.

Now here are some other features of this metaphor that I want you to consider in the case of people and their contexts:

- *Scientists do not really understand how this stuff with mobiles actually happens in terms of particles*. They know what happens in practice (as waves) and can manipulate and change that and get all our mobile phones tuned and working, but the nitty-gritty is unclear. Their equations do a remarkable job of predicting how to make mobiles work but *interpreting* those equations has been a problem. For example, unlike ripples in a pond there is no medium for the electromagnetic waves to move through, since such waves can somehow move through a vacuum. Physicists will instead say that there is an 'electromagnetic field' set up by magnetism and electricity through your mobile phone, and even name it as a 'force' or say that 'energy' is propagated in that field, but the detailed meanings of these words are all murky.
- My point, then, is that ***we do not need to know the minute details of how social contexts affect us in order to rethink and make changes***. Mobile phones work pretty well considering we do not understand

all the detail. So going back to Chapter 1, in order to understand how all the contexts in which we are immersed can influence us, we do not have to wait for all the particle details in the old sequential, causal chain of:

light → sense organs → brain → 'processing' → memory → retrieval → response.

- *We do not see the electromagnetic waves from the mobiles and they act 'at a distance'*. They are invisible and act over long distances, yet this all really happens. Likewise, just because someone is not present does not mean they are not influencing us, and it is better (as I am suggesting to you) to think of such external social contexts as affecting us at a distance rather than trying to 'explain' these influences by means of an internal storage area of the brain or an elaborate causal chain involving particles that are purely hypothetical anyway (i.e. make a good story).
- *Electromagnetic waves do not work causally as billiard balls which bounce the cause on to the next object and thereby have their influence*. Rather, they permeate at a distance, usually, and the context or arrangement of their presence brings about any outcomes depending on what those contexts are. If the tower is empty then nothing happens in the context of those waves. If there is a receiver 'attuned' in particular ways *then signals will emerge from that context* which can be relayed, sent back to the sender, etc. We can send a different frequency of electromagnetic waves to that tower and nothing will eventuate because it is not 'attuned'. Aim your microwave oven at a receiving/transmission tower and nothing happens. Notice, however, that we still need to know a lot more about how people are attuned to their social and historical (Plasticine) contexts in life. The metaphor alone will not give you those descriptions – there is still hard work to do.
- *The influence of many electromagnetic waves can be at the same place and yet act in non-interfering ways, and also not in an obvious additive collision fashion that makes a big mess in the tower's circuits*. Likewise, I have described the multiple, contextual influences as all lurking externally but not interfering with one another directly. The waves (contextual influences, 'fields' of influence) are not inside us nor are they in the external objects. They are in the contexts of the relations between context and person – what Kantor called 'interbehavioral' and Bentley called 'transdermal'.
- *The tower receiving the waves does not have to 'see' the waves; there is an influence if there is a relational attunement.* In fact, to move to

fantasy briefly, the receiving/transmission tower receiving the waves probably thinks it is generating the attunements and transmission by its own 'decision-making processes' or 'cognitive processes' just as we do! (Yes, this bit is just useful fiction, but will be interesting when considering in Chapter 4 what is going on when we have a strong sense that our thoughts control our behavior. A talkative tower might say the same thing …)

These are the parameters of the electromagnetic wave analogy I want to work with. Once again, I am not trying to say that we influence each other's 'minds' by electromagnetic waves or even some energy wave of the 'Vulcan mind meld' variety from Star Trek. It is just a metaphor to show you that you can rethink common ways of thinking about our world and what influences what, and resist the causal, particle, stimulus/response, sequential processing, real-time decision-making types of thinking currently employed when trying to understand people.

Imagine you are sitting quietly reading and suddenly you get up and go get a biscuit, and you might even surprise yourself doing this. If asked why you got up just then, we all have stock answers to use, such as, "Well, I obviously was hungry." But we do not really know what happened. And my point is that to trace all the particle connections is not worth the effort even if it could be done. The event might not even be about hunger. The context could, as an example, be about avoiding reading any more of this book.

What we can do more usefully is to describe all the contexts past and present related to the event, the people involved, and through these descriptions find out what contexts were influencing you, what have been consequences in the past, and what you have become attuned to when sitting quietly reading. For example, it might be that you have in the past suddenly got up for food when you are losing sight of the plot of the book and are avoiding looking (to imagined audiences perhaps) like an idiot who cannot read properly. It might, in such a case, be entirely irrelevant whether you get a biscuit or a sandwich. If you were actually hungry, your contexts might normally lead to a longer lag time from when you rehearse thoughts about eating (while you are trying to read), rather than a sudden arising. A contextual analysis would show us possible distinctions between such occurrences, which can then be researched more systematically.

One criticism people still have, however, is that we do not *really* understand anything until we have the causal, particle, version of an explanation. This is why we need a new metaphor right now to get us out of this thinking trap.

Metaphor 5. We can utilize gravity even if physicists do not understand how it works

Sir Isaac Newton produced his three laws of motion and Kepler used astronomical data to show that these laws of motion could very closely predict the orbits of the planets around the Sun. Since the 1950s, scientists at NASA and elsewhere have used the forces of gravity to swing rocket probes and spaceships around the Moon in trajectories that bring them back safely to Earth. Many countries can now place satellites in orbits around the Earth so the breakaway acceleration matches the gravitational pull of the Earth on those satellites and they stay in an orbit.

Big deal. Why am I telling you this? We obviously understand gravity really well since it is used regularly and reliably by physicists and space engineers. We can send people in spaceships towards the Moon and then use the Moon's gravity to swing the spaceship precisely around so it either orbits the Moon or comes back to Earth.

Well, the problem with this, which is the reason for me telling you all this, is that we can 'understand' gravity perfectly well in some practical ways, but physicists really do not have much idea about how any of that works in terms of either causes and particles or even waves and contextual attunement! Two bodies attract each other, but why? How? Newton just said they did, and provided an accurate equation (outside of quantum mechanics). Einstein said that space-time bends or curves and gravity occurs in those contexts. But we still do not know how or why this happens (Clegg, 2012). Here is a recent summary from the Web (www.howstuffworks.com/question232.htm):

> Still more-recent theories of gravity express the phenomenon in terms of particles and waves. One view states that particles called gravitons cause objects to be attracted to one another. Gravitons have never actually been observed, though. And neither have *gravitational waves*, sometimes called gravitational radiation, which supposedly are generated when an object is accelerated by an external force.

This metaphor is to get you thinking that something as well known and utilized as gravity is not at all understood, yet we can carry on. It happens at a distance although no particles or fields have ever been detected or measured. Similarly, we can also 'understand' how mobile phones emit electromagnetic waves (not particles) which influence any nearby receiving/transmission tower which is attuned to that wave, but we do not know how this all occurs. And finally (the metaphor bit), we can perfectly 'understand' in one sense how people's behavior emerges from the contexts they are in and have been in before (and been changed by that), and 'understand' how this is best thought of as action-at-a-distance and not as causal chains, but, and here is the big but, we can do all this even before we know how the brain and all the senses work as particles in causal chains.

The problem I see is that those explaining or understanding people's actions have known that the brain and senses must be involved and have therefore been thinking that to be proper and plausible, their understanding *must* be couched in particle/causal/detailed/cellular-level words. Not so.

My argument, and I am trying to help you think this with the gravity metaphor, is that we can fully 'understand' and get on with helping people think of actions in terms of contexts affecting us by resonating at a distance as it were, and us having multiple effects from that which do not have to interfere. So, the metaphoric message is, once again like in Chapter 1, not to worry about filling in causal chains as if that were the only way we can 'understand' people. The contextual way of understanding people is one way (there might be others, I am sure) to get on with things without waiting for links to the senses and brain cells. Worst of all, thinking in those ways, as I tried to demonstrate metaphorically in Chapter 1, leads us to be looking at the wrong things and trying to measure artificial things that come from abstract words and theories rather than contextual experience and observation.

The point of these two metaphors, then, is that if we can rid ourselves (following Chapter 1) of thinking causally and sequentially, with no more billiard ball particles colliding to cause the next part of the chain, then we can begin thinking that there are social and other contexts we are attuned to (as consequences of past experience) and that in those contexts we behave in certain ways.

And my real point for metaphors is that in the early part of the twentieth century this is exactly what quantum physicists were trying to do. They know how to do this better now, even if they still do not know how it all works exactly. They can make towers receive (attune) and transmit (respond by passing on) without knowing the exact details from the 50 mobile phones on the bus to the transmission. They can shoot spaceships around the Moon and across the galaxy (like the Voyagers) but not really understand how gravity works or what it is, except as waves. I will not go into their current ways of thinking about nuclear events since there are no particles anyway and it in no way 'looks like' anything we deal with in our life (Cox & Forshaw, 2011) – but the properties of light, subatomic events, and the like can no longer be envisaged as we do the objects around us. And yet these people are the 'hard' scientists!

The biggest point probably from all this metaphoric changing of thinking is that we are influenced by other people and contexts in myriad ways even when those people are not there. Just because someone is not there does not mean that they are not influencing us. And in turn this means that *we can have ubiquitous and constant social contexts influencing everything we do even without people being there*. What I am trying to get across to you is that a good way to start thinking about this is that they are acting on us like waves do (resonating) in multitudes without us seeing them, and we do not have to propose some particles that are present to represent their influence.

To help with these two points of invisibility and multitudes, consider the following two fictitious examples of things people frequently say that sometimes seem ridiculous if thought of in terms of particles. These examples relate most closely to Chapter 1 (the first one) and Chapter 4 (the second one):

> "It just seemed like there was this invisible pressure to do certain things and not do some others that part of me wanted to do. It was like a powerful force making me go through the motions but I couldn't see where it was coming from. I guess I just blamed myself for having these pressures."
>
> (Someone stressing out over their life but not knowing what these pressures actually are or where they are coming from)

> "It was like a thousand voices somewhere telling me to do everything and explain and make excuses. Like a real pressure coming from nowhere. Not even voices that I could sort of hear; just something in between."
>
> (Someone hearing voices that have a real influence on them but they are not able to articulate this in terms of causal/particle explanations so it seems unreal somehow, and is not taken seriously by others)

We still have one more link to make, however, so we can think both that everything we do is influenced by other people and that despite the fact we cannot immediately see this influence, it is still very real. I have been using the term 'attunement' for how the contexts influence us rather than causal chains, just as the receiving/transmission tower was attuned to respond to certain mobile phones.

To make this clearer I will offer a new metaphor for attunement as well, so you can get a feel for how this is also a new way of thinking. Hopefully you got the basic idea from physics, that when our televisions 'pick up' the signals being sent as waves, there are no particles flying around the room and hitting the television and us. Rather, there are electromagnetic waves from the receiving/transmission tower that change the electromagnetic coils inside the television but only those that are attuned to 'pick up' those waves.

But to help us think about language use, and in Chapter 4 think about our thoughts and thinking itself, we probably need a better metaphor. For this rethinking of *attunement* rather than particles causing events through collisions, I will use *sympathetic resonance*.

Metaphor 6. Think of attunement as sympathetic resonance

You might be familiar with sympathetic resonance but most people are not. For example, if you pluck a string on a guitar which is close to another guitar, and the two are *perfectly tuned* to each other (attuned), then the same string on the second guitar will start vibrating without you even touching it – that is sympathetic resonance. It is likely that the first guitar will also resonate the octave of the base note, the fifth, the next major third up, etc. – all the harmonics as well on the second guitar. In fact, one string plucked on one guitar will also resonate on itself the octave of the base note, the fifth, the next major third up, etc., called standing waves.

Likewise, if you hit one piano key and have all the rest open (pedal pressed down), you will hear the resonating octaves, fifth, third, etc., but not on a digital piano, of course. Great piano composers know this and write accordingly so as to include resonating harmonics on other strings to enter the piece of music as part of the sound while not being explicitly written in the music. And finally, Indian sitars have 12–14 sympathetic strings that are never plucked at all, but which only ever resonate with the 6–7 main plucked strings.

There are some interesting properties of this for us, properties which resemble the electromagnetic waves we have been talking about so far (not surprising, since sound waves and electromagnetic waves share most wave properties, except that sound needs air for a medium). A key property is that this can happen at a distance. I can have one guitar on one side of the room, the other guitar on the other side, and we can still get resonance under the right conditions if one guitar is attuned to the other perfectly. This works and actually happens. Try it to make sure I am not messing with you. Any acoustic instrument will do.

So I want this metaphor to get you thinking in terms of *contexts relevant to our past and present producing (fictitious) waves, like giant standing waves, and if we are properly attuned to those contexts from our past experiences and perhaps even some hard-wiring, then we resonate or respond* – but not in a causal billiard-balls-hitting fashion, and not in a sensation-leads-to-perception cognitive model way, either. Many of them will be resonating at any one time, without them all interfering.

For the present chapter, this means we can try thinking as if the ubiquitous social contexts in our lives produce waves and that most of what we do is attuned to these social waves and resonates, with only some waves leading to actions. When we get to Chapter 4 and thinking, we will see that any contextual event also resonates with language-use actions to produce lots of language responding, most of which is not formulated, edited, rehearsed, or even said out loud (this is what we call thinking, actually). But those thoughts are better imagined as out there in the contexts rather than inside our heads, and this is what the sympathetic resonance metaphor can help us understand.

From my first example above, if we were only to observe the second guitar without its context (the first guitar), it would certainly seem to spontaneously begin vibrating, because nothing at all touched it! Imagine filming the second guitar up close with no sound, and so you cannot see the first guitar being plucked. It will seem as if the second guitar magically begins to vibrate, just as we seem to magically begin to think about people we have not seen for a while. But in terms of contexts resonating unexpectedly and from hidden places, this makes sense. You should now be able to 'think this'!

To further help your rethinking, you might also want to try these examples of resonance:

- http://www.youtube.com/watch?v=zWKiWaiM3Pw
- http://www.youtube.com/watch?v=i-4Qw9-Lnr8
- http://www.youtube.com/watch?v=zVqvd6mhat8

- http://www.youtube.com/watch?v=wYoxOJDrZzw
- http://video.mit.edu/watch/tuning-forks-resonance-a-beat-frequency-11447
- http://www.youtube.com/watch?v=jwLWmhGrdBU.

Twelve ways that being alone is social: how can we think that?

To make this more realistic and concrete, now that I have tried to shift your thinking about the ubiquitous social influences on people, I want to suggest some more specific metaphorical ways to think about this social context influencing us like electromagnetic waves resonating through a transmission tower which is attuned. I will focus by looking at ways in which a situation is still a social one even when we are alone – that is, even at a temporal or spatial distance. I will suggest 12 ways to think about all human behavior as socially contextualized.

For this section, imagine someone alone in a room playing a guitar. *How can this be a social situation or context? How can we even think that?* For many of these points below, I will use this example of someone playing their guitar alone in a room. (This was an example someone gave to me once as proof that social control is not ubiquitous, since the person playing guitar alone in the room is 'obviously' determining everything and there is nothing social about it. My response to them included a lot of what follows.)

I am hoping the '12 ways in which being alone is social' will get you thinking about being alone as a fully social context even though there are no social billiard ball particles (i.e. people, social contexts) present at the time. This will begin to show how all our actions, even the most 'inner', have a social basis – even our most private thoughts and actions are saturated in the social (the point mentioned above that Wittgenstein missed). To help your thinking, you can think of these 12 social contexts as having an influence in a metaphorically similar way to waves having their influence. If you can get all these points then you will be able to make better contextual observations of human behavior in the social context because you will know the subtle social events to look for and to ask about when trying to understand why people do what they do.

(If you have trouble thinking this, go and stand at a nearby radio/mobile tower and notice that nothing is happening and it seems all alone and shutdown – then remember that thousands of waves are resonating at any one time through this tower. Then, when you next see someone alone in a room playing the guitar, remember that they are not really separate from their social contexts at all, just because you cannot see anything.)

(1) The contexts for acting are almost all provided by other people, even when one is alone

Our first contextual observation must be that everything about our lives is there because of other people. At present I am sitting at a table in a cafeteria at another university, drinking coffee and working on a laptop computer. We do not normally observe this, but everything about this situation (even though I am obviously alone and working quietly 'by myself') was brought about by other people and is still dependent upon other people. For example, if the people running this cafeteria realized I was not part of their university I might be thrown out since it is for their university's staff and students only.

This point needs emphasizing. For example, I am also about to eat a banana as a snack and the banana is surely nature's own produce. But how did it get here, get grown, made economically viable, who purchased it for me, who packed it in my bag, etc.? Even a natural banana is part of my context only because of a whole slew of other people who could interfere or change things at any time.

When we observe people acting in situations, we almost never 'see' these social contexts; but, like electromagnetic waves, they are always there influencing outcomes. We tend to observe those things and events which stand out from their background. However, as mentioned in the previous chapter, naming things or events that stand out as causes is an artificial practice and not a contextual way to view life. We also saw earlier that Arthur Bentley pointed out a long time ago that our whole way of talking about 'seeing' is biased in this way. When we talk of 'seeing' we are biased towards 'seeing' things and events in a cross-sectional way – "I saw the blue bird" – rather than over time and space – "I saw the blue bird fly in a parabolic flight and land on the branch." We have been trained to 'see' causally (particles) rather than contextually (waves)!

In another example which is more obviously full of hidden social contexts, Bentley (1935) imagined the scene of a conference of scientists in a hall. He wanted to be able to 'see' through the *spaces*, in the sense that everything there extends beyond the immediate hall, the transport to get there, the families, the congress budget, etc. It also extends beyond the particular *time*, to the preparation, the writing of congress papers, etc. It also extends beyond the immediate *lives* of the scientists, to their education and research programs, their reputations, their families again, etc.

> If, as a surface surveyor, I should now attempt to frame my exhibit solely within the walls of the room, the week of the meeting, and the living of those present, it would be to show myself painfully deficient in skill. My approach would be no better that that of an investigator of rivers who, finding a level stretch of stream bed, would attempt his examination with eyes closed to the fall of the land above and below.
>
> Again, if I should concentrate all of my attention upon some one fascinating feature of the situation, my approach would be scarcely better .... Our obligation, therefore, is to keep alert to all that we can find and have power to see, and see it all as set within its wide frames of progression.
>
> (Bentley, 1935, p. 141)

As mentioned, this is difficult to do in practice since we are trained otherwise. Bentley goes on to illustrate this point:

> If, in conversation with a friend, I chance to remark upon the visibility of the social, he will be quite sure to smile as he replies: "Its invisibility is what you mean." He will talk to me fluently about society and its events, usually with much more confidence and assurance than I can show. But as for actually 'seeing' the social, that is another matter.

Bentley focuses on the verb 'to see'. 'Seeing' can be transitive or intransitive, although Bentley limits discussion to the transitive uses only, when there is an 'object' being seen. The intransitive use implies capacities and often mental assumptions: 'I can see', 'I perceive.' "It is this full behavioral event, inclusive of both the 'seeing' and the 'seen,' with which we must concern ourselves" (p. 200). I have referred to these as 'causal seeing' and 'contextual seeing' and we obviously need to focus more on the skills needed to carry out the latter since people are rarely skilled at this.

> The organism, of course, seems in everyday life and language to stand out strongly apart from the transactions in which it is engaged. This is a superficial observation. One reason for it is that the organism is engaged in so many transactions.
>
> (Dewey & Bentley, 1949, p. 138)

What this amounts to is that if you cannot 'see' the social context of almost everything we do and what is around us then this is more a statement about your own limited 'transitive observational' or 'contextual observational' skills, not a comment on reality! If you can only observe the objects/particles immediately around you to find out what is influencing what, then you will have a limited view of reality. You will also have a limited understanding of the things and events we talk about commonly as spiritual, cultural, or mystical. These do not refer to mysterious extra-reality 'things' as is often imagined but to transitive observational events that are very real. Just because they are not limited to a particular time and space does not mean that they are mysterious things, but merely transitive and not often observed by 'non-spirited' persons.

(2) Social development and scaffolding of human actions

A second way that acting alone can be seen as social comes through the development of our behavior. All of those behaviors that are eventually explained as 'individual' or 'personal' have enormous social shaping from a young age. With careful observations over time of the social context, it can usually be found that this social shaping remains in a different form or, as behavior analysts discuss it, on a much leaner or intermittent social scheduling.

Developmental psychologists have a nice term for this that I will slightly change from their usage: *social scaffolding* (Connor, Knight, & Cross, 1997; Landry, Garner, Swank, & Baldwin, 1996; Wood, Bruner, & Ross, 1976). The behaviors of children have a scaffold of adult social consequences. That is, *children's behavior is mostly shaped with parental social behavior as the consequence rather than the outcomes of what is done*. Even the attentional focus of young children is guided, that is, shaped, by parents and caregivers. For example, children look at things and all the while they are looking back to their parents to get the effects or consequences that will maintain looking: *the consequences or effects that maintain looking do not come from what they are looking at but from the effects on people* (Franco & Butterworth, 1996; Hains & Muir, 1996; Smith, Landry, Miller-Loncar, & Swank, 1997). Social constructionists might say that patterns of looking and attention are not a physiological given but are socially constructed.

Although it might seem that we grow out of this 'visual checking with a social partner' (Franco & Butterworth, 1996) as we get older, I suggest instead that the audience changes from parents to significant others, but not the social scaffolding of behavior itself (Mead, 1934), and that the 'looking back to the parents' changes into rehearsals of stories to tell others (this is expanded in Chapter 4). Our whole systems of preferences of looking, even in adulthood, can be viewed as relying on or being maintained by a history with other people. For example, what we look at as adults is for talking or thinking about later, and both these are social, as will be shown in Chapters 3 and 4. The social scaffold equivalents for adults are socially constructed stories, excuses, jokes, and accounts.

Another example of this is so-called 'intrinsic' motivation. An activity based on intrinsic motivation is said to be one for which there *appear to be* no external consequences maintaining the behavior. Typically, the tasks in such experiments involve puzzles and toys that children play with alone, seemingly without adult intervention or obvious consequences. Adding 'obvious' rewards or reinforcement on top even seems to weaken the behavior under some conditions, and this has been taken as evidence against crude reinforcement theories.

But we need to ask what has guided our doing something that supposedly has no consequences; why do children continue to play with the puzzles that are used in the intrinsic motivation research in the first place? Cognitive psychologists might agree that such 'intrinsically interesting' tasks start off with social reinforcement or social scaffolding, but they believe that this fades to individualistic or agency control. I would argue that the social outcomes just become more difficult to see and less reliant on specific people such as the parents.

The problem is not one of doubting that the phenomena associated with 'intrinsic motivation' exist. The problem is one of both sides refusing to delve more intensively into the historical and social contexts for what seems to be 'intrinsic'. Cognitive psychologists must move beyond acquiescing in talk of 'intrinsic' motivations and needs, and behavior analysts must move beyond the sole use of simple schedules of reinforcement when analyzing such social behaviors. If both can carry out analyses and contextual observations of the full historical and social contexts, this will get us beyond internecine disputes, whether or not my specific suggestions are accurate.

So the real problem that is raised by the example of 'intrinsic motivation' is in the behavior and language of the researchers rather than anything the children do when playing. The cognitive psychologists and others acquiesce to allow an unexplained need or motivation simply labeled 'intrinsic'. The behavior analysts acquiesce in the simple schedules of reinforcement and have not begun explicating the complex and historical shaping of children playing with toys alone in their room (which presumably develops into guitar- and game-playing alone when they become teenagers).

Merely as one suggestion to help us begin looking for the social contexts of seemingly 'intrinsically motivated' play, parents have probably put some considerable effort into shaping their children to play alone so that they do not need full parental attention, given that parents have so much else to do. This social shaping is simply ignored by both sides of the dispute. Until both sides begin analyzing what exactly is going on to achieve the 'intrinsic' or seemingly unreinforced performance, we will not get much closer to an answer. This standoff arises commonly because both sides of a dispute typically ignore the full contexts of what is happening and come up with abstract words to use in what is really an unknown situation. In this way, the other social sciences are often well ahead of psychology, because they frequently use methods of long and intensive observation.

(3) Childhood actions that were developed with 'social scaffolding' remain in adulthood but become hard to observe

To make this more specific, all of the most important verbal or cognitive functional activities of adults have been suggested, or shown, to have their control in social contexts. These include visual attention (Bakeman & Adamson, 1984; Collis & Shaffer, 1975; Corkum & Moore, 1998; Moore, Angelopoulos, & Bennett, 1997; Saxon, Frick, & Colombo, 1997), eye contact (Peláez-Nogueras et al., 1996, 1997), 'theory of mind' (verbal behavior using mentalistic concepts; Watson, Nixon, Wilson, & Capage, 1999), imitation (Ugiris, 1991), reciprocity (Brazelton, Koslowski, & Main, 1974; Dunham, Dunham, Tran, & Aktar, 1991; Papousek, 1995; Ratner & Bruner, 1978; Roe & Drivas, 1997), language (Baldwin, 1993; Baldwin & Markman, 1989; Bloom, 1975; Bloom, Russell, & Wassenberg, 1987; Dunham & Dunham, 1992; Dunham, Dunham, & Curwin, 1993; Masur, 1982; Ninio & Bruner, 1977; Tomasello & Farrar, 1986), referential communication (Butterworth & Grover, 1988; Franco & Butterworth, 1996; Leung & Rheingold, 1981; Trevarthen, 1979), meta-cognition (verbal behavior about verbal behavior; Karabenick, 1996), motivation (Wood et al., 1976), exploration (Messer, 1978), self-regulation (Halle & Shatz, 1994), and other cognitive operations (Azmitia & Hesser, 1993; Carugati & Gilly, 1993; Doise, Mugny, & Perret-Clermont, 1975; Monteil & Huguet, 1999).

(4) Developmentally, the major skills of thinking and cognition are learned and supported through social scaffolding or social control

Putting these last two points together suggests that thinking itself will be socially controlled, unless we need to posit that some 'inner agency' develops out of the scaffolding. In Chapter 4 this will be spelled out in more detail, how the very thinking about ourselves and others depends upon audiences. For now, just start imagining this is true – that whenever we think, this activity has contexts brought about by other people and is about other people. It is not about controlling your future actions. The next chapter will also help you conceptualize how the tight social controls over language use seen in development remain for social control for adults.

(5) *We have ways of conceptualizing social control functioning over time and space*

This was a question for Chapter 1: that many of the problems of not seeing social control when alone come from thinking causally rather than contextually. In this way, we want to link causally the social events to the alone events by a causal/particle chain: usually sensations → perception → memory → cognition → remote social influence. This way of thinking greatly limits our understanding. There have, however, been several ways previously suggested in Chapter 1 for thinking more contextually, thereby 'seeing' a direct social influence even when no one else is present. These are in addition to all my metaphors.

In behavior analysis, for example, contingency control can function over time and space, or can be conceptualized as 'transdermal' (Bentley, 1935, 1941; Lee, 1992). Therefore, there is not the problem that most psychology has about acting alone being social when no one else happens to be there (cf. Guerin, 1993). For example, avoidance contingencies still work even when the punisher is not there, providing that the social context has been arranged properly.

In fact, the opposite argument can be made. If I am sitting alone in my room but still socially controlled, this must involve powerful forms of social control to be effective with no one there to monitor. All control can be intermittent and work over long time periods, especially if generalized social contingencies are doing the shaping.

Similarly we saw earlier how Bentley (1935) put this well when describing how most science treats observations as the observation of things, as in "I saw a bird." Instead, Bentley urged that in science we need also to take seriously the form "I saw a bird fly right across the lake," in which the 'thing' seen is spread across time and space and is not a simple object – what I called *contextual observation*. Both forms are acceptable, but the concentration has been on the former. Once the second form of observing statements is allowed, someone alone in a room can more easily be 'seen' as a conglomerate of social interactions, and it makes little difference whether those other people happen to be there or not. In this way, we can truly say that we observe individuals in their social relationships and that our 'self' is spread over our relationships even if the others are not present.

Finally, if none of those other ways satisfies you to think about social control when alone, then use the wave and resonance/attunement ideas.

(6) Doing things to yourself is itself learned as a social behavior

There are many references in the literature that doing things to yourself is also learned as a social behavior, activities such as talking to yourself and developing ideas (telling stories) about your 'self' (Cast, Stets, & Burke, 1999; Mead, 1934; Miller, Potts, Fung, Hoogstra, & Mintz, 1990; Skinner, 1957). Lodhi and Greer (1989) gave some evidence for this, with children's talking to themselves shown as a variant form of talking to others. It also takes time for children to learn to work alone. As another example, Manne (1999) found that the intrusive negative thoughts of cancer patients, usually considered to be highly individual and internal, were controlled and perhaps initiated by actions of their spouses. For example, some patients had learned to avoid hearing their spouse's criticism 'in their heads' with intrusive thoughts.

Some other examples were given above and more of this will be spelled out in Chapter 4 when we look at how we think and how we think about ourselves, and how to conceptualize these as social events. The point here is that when we do things to ourselves, talk to ourselves, or think about ourselves, these are also social events even when we are completely alone.

(7) You can act as if alone while in the presence of others

Being alone is so socially controlled that you can even act as if alone while in the presence of others. I can go to a party I do not wish to attend and, in my grandiose grouchiness, act like I am all alone and not involved. But notice that the context even for doing this is highly social. This again suggests that 'aloneness' is an arrangement of social contexts, not a state of mind. It is socially controlled. This also makes it easier to view being alone as a social activity, in that the social control of either being alone or being with others can be seen more obviously as social events.

(8) Acting alone in some cases emerges from a social context of avoidance or escape

Avoidance of others is a common social situation, and acting alone may in some cases be socially controlled by avoidance (Billig, 2001; Goffman,

1967). What this means, as explained elsewhere (Guerin, 2004), is that the behaviors that are actually done when one is alone might be totally irrelevant to the obvious current contexts in any case. I am being alone in my room to avoid going in the other room because there is someone I wish to avoid.

The practical problem is that when avoidance like this is successful, we do not *see* in the most immediate context whatever is being avoided (since it does not eventuate), and so the activity that is actually being engaged in can be over-interpreted. We see someone playing a guitar alone in a room and attribute this behavior to reasons involving that person and the music, such as their extreme liking for the guitar. However, the person may actually be avoiding someone in the next room she or he dislikes, and what we actually see the person doing can be otherwise irrelevant to the avoidance (they needed to do something to indicate that they should not be disturbed so they happened to grab the guitar and start playing). We also need to be careful in analyzing human social behavior to take such events into account, and this is another way that acting alone can be social. It is also another reason for carrying out longer historical observations of people before claiming that their activities are understood.

Avoidance is just one example of this. Acting alone could also function socially because in the past someone has sought you out when you stayed by yourself. This might encourage playing music alone in some instances, to get attention. In variations of this involving language once more, being alone could maintain someone coming to find you and asking you to explain yourself or talk about what you were doing, thus allowing an opportunity for reputation-enhancing activities or impression-management strategies of telling stories: "Oh, glad you happened to ask. I was playing the guitar piece I will play at the major museum opening next week. Did I mention I was invited to solo for that?" There are probably many variations of social strategies along these lines.

(9) It is in people's best interest to disguise the social control of their own behavior

A large amount of the sociological and social anthropological research on secrecy and anonymity, of which being alone is one example and wearing a veil is another, suggests that it is in people's best interest to be able to disguise the social control of their own behavior (Bailey, 1991; Cohen, 1971; El Guindi, 1999; Erickson, 1981; Herdt, 1990; Keen, 1994; Merten, 1999; Murphy, 1964; Read & Bartkowski, 2000; Richardson, 1988; Simmel, 1950; Tetlock & Manstead, 1985).

There are systematic and strategic uses of secrecy and withdrawal in social life, mapped out carefully by social anthropologists, emphasizing that being alone is a social event when considered in terms of the local and historical social contexts. It is not the case, then, that it is somehow 'natural' to be alone, that aloneness thus does not need any explanation, or that the explanation is simply a 'desire' of the person, whereas being with others demands an explanation. Indeed, for most groups around the world, other than Westernized groups, being alone can be considered either rude or very odd. Whatever the details of any particular group and social context, changing from open to secretive, or from sociable to aloof, strategically helps negotiate our group resources and confirms the idea that any acting alone is socially controlled and can be changed by changing the social contexts. It is a very Western way of thinking to assume that individuals acting alone are the natural units and then seek to explain why people come together. Elsewhere, being alone is what demands an explanation:

> For a person to wish to be alone means that he is either antisocial or ashamed. The word for doing something off by oneself means 'stealth' and connotes activities that are either embarrassing or intended to be clandestine.
>
> (Schieffelin, 1976, p. 151, writing about the Kaluli tribe of New Guinea)

> The concept of an individual alone in a tribal religious sense is ridiculous. The very complexity of tribal life and the interdependence of people on one another makes this concept improbable at best, a terrifying loss of identity at worst.
>
> (Deloria, 1994, p. 195)

(10) Being able to be alone is indicative of certain lifestyle, cultural, socioeconomic, and class circumstances

Taking the previous point (9) further, if someone is able to spend time alone in a room playing a guitar, this by itself is enough to give a clue about the cultural and socioeconomic contexts of that person. In many parts of the world, such activities might be considered a luxury available only to the wealthy. In many parts of the world, the social organization is such that people would not wish to be alone but with others of their kin or community; as already mentioned, being alone would be considered rude or deviant in many communities. In many parts of the world, being alone might even be considered aversive and might be used more as a punishment than a luxury for the wealthy.

Whichever of these apply, the point is that being alone is not an automatic or 'natural' state for any person, a sort of baseline condition determined by our individualistic or psychological makeup; rather, it is already a strategic part of social life. If people can play their guitar alone, then this depends on all of the cultural, socioeconomic, and class contexts (structural opportunities) available to them. This makes any form of being alone, anywhere in the world, socially controlled; it cannot happen just anywhere but needs particular social contexts to emerge. The social is ubiquitous.

(11) Doing things alone to earn money later is social

Most things that we use now have money as a precondition, enabling event, or setting event. In the same way as was argued for language, money also is completely social and has no consequences outside of a social context (Simmel, 1907/1978). Without a stable economic system and other people, money would have no effects in the world. From this it follows that making music alone in our example, or doing almost anything else alone, can be done to earn money later and therefore has a social context: change the economics, and the behavior would also change in some ways; for example, change to barter, and the whole organization of social relationships changes (Görlich, 1998; Hart, 1986; Thomas, 1992). So there are social contexts such as money that resonate even when we are alone.

(12) The notions of a private life, aloneness, and agency are themselves useful conversational rhetoric or strategies that pervade Western society and Western social science thinking

The final point brings together some ideas offered in different ways throughout, that the whole way we conceptualize talking, explaining, making stories, and instructing people in terms of being located in a 'mental' domain or a private, 'inner' self are *conversational strategies in themselves* with considerable power to influence others, and the social sciences have uncritically taken these on board. What this means is that talking in terms of 'inner' control, a person's 'depths', and 'mental' domains is itself a way of talking that has rhetorical properties. Primarily, these ways of talking by psychologists and others are abstract, can be persuasive, and are very difficult to refute since they are so abstract.

Psychology, especially, has taken these strategies as its very domain of expertise (the experts in assessing and dealing with 'mental' issues) without recognizing that their social and conversational basis is really in the talk of psychologists trying to convince people of facts (Guerin, 2001; Rose, 1996). This is why psychology, unlike most sciences, has been able to go through huge changes (fads) in theories and perspectives without being embarrassed by such shifts (Innes, 1980). There is generally a gradual acquiescence in going along with the new fads in theorizing.

The conversational properties of talking in terms of a hidden, inner domain (rather than talking about social contexts) are very powerful if used strategically, and some suggestions are given below:

- Positive outcome strategies for speakers talking in terms of their own inner world include: such talk cannot be monitored or verified; it can be changed by claiming that an inner change has occurred; it is abstract talk that allows for easy hedging; and it allows full explanations to be avoided, which is especially important if the 'real' causes are unknown even to the speaker. For example, if arguing that we should go to the beach rather than a movie, we can say, "But I really *don't feel like* seeing a movie right now." Replying "Yes you do" seems weird. This makes it difficult for the listener to monitor, evaluate, and challenge this unless they are monitoring over time in terms of consistency, "But you always prefer the movies to the beach!"
- Negative outcome strategies for such speakers include the possibility that consistency in what is said becomes emphasized as the way to monitor the 'truth' of what is going on (although this can be easily hedged by most speakers), that people might not take what is said seriously (much as the early behaviorists did), that people might avoid someone who uses this strategy constantly, and that the real world might catch up with the stories.

The point here, therefore, is that the whole notion and ways of talking about being truly alone, of talking to oneself, of having private inner beliefs, feelings, and attitudes, can be seen as social conversational strategies that have developed and which people learn to use in context. Again, being alone is not the 'natural' state.

When making explanations or stories about *other* people (rather than ourselves) that utilize an inner domain, the strategies for a speaker are similar: others can be made responsible or be blamed, and there are no verifiable checks they can provide to counter this; a label can be attached within this 'inner' world that can then be talked about as if real (e.g. dispositional attributions); and, finally, because there are no verifiable checks on what is said by either the speaker or someone else about this 'inner' domain, an authoritative power can appoint people to be socially responsible for adjudicating what really goes on 'inside' people. This can have both good and bad outcomes, of course, and adjudicators have historically included shamans, psychiatrists, and psychologists (Foucault, 1978, 1988; Riches, 1994; Rose, 1996; Taussig, 1987).

It is interesting that *social consistency* becomes the substitute method for monitoring 'truth' when people's talk (metaphors) turns abstract and starts referring to inner worlds and mental domains. I cannot 'see into your soul' to find out whether you are telling the truth so I have to monitor your consistency – do you start telling me different things another time? The problem is that this can encourage people to act as if they are highly consistent (to appease others), even though consistency can be maladaptive in a changing environment and consistency is no guide to correctness anyway. This no doubt strengthens the conversational use of consistent identity stories as causes and also increases caution in saying and doing too much that is concrete, because others might find inconsistencies (Yngvesson & Mahoney, 2000). It also emphasizes that verbal ability becomes a powerful social tool or social capital.

In summary, the very individualistic and mentalistic way of talking that supports 'aloneness' as private and non-social, can itself be looked at as a ubiquitous conversational social strategy, and so the reader's reticence to think about someone's being alone as social behavior might be further assuaged. Such individualistic or mentalistic talk has many useful properties for gaining resources through convincing people of 'facts' and being able to resist counter-arguments. This has been made worse in that the 'facts' being talked about (the true causes or contexts for human actions) are not easily amenable because of their generalized nature, even to those performing the actions. This has allowed a century of easy theorizing based on cross-sectional measurements. The hard contextual work is still to come.

How do social relationships pervade our actions, thinking, and self-thinking?

My belief is that we have only just begun to understand how the ubiquities of social relationships pervade all our actions. Moving from requiring a particle/causal metaphor to a wave/contextual resonance metaphor is my way of guiding you through this. Chapters 3 and 4 have a lot more to say about the social contexts for language use, thinking, and self-thinking but here I wish to briefly outline some guiding thoughts on this question.

As the quotations from Arthur Bentley at the beginning of this chapter hint, the ubiquity of social influence on everything human has always been a murky problem for psychology. It is usually dealt with by positing the building of social representations that cognitively mediate relations in the world, or by vaguely suggesting social 'motives' for behavior such as 'need for approval', 'social desirability', or 'conformity to norms'. But these are most often dragged in only when the social influences are obvious ones; explanations based on 'inner determinants' prevail in other cases.

There are two main elements to seeing the social everywhere, which will be brought together in Chapter 5 after more details have been spelled out. The *first* is to see the full social basis to language use in social behavior and then how language use pervades most social behavior, and the *second* is to see how our other actions rely on social relationships. I will leave the first aside until Chapter 3.

A start can be made on recognizing the way social relationships pervade our behaviors by extending the points made above about the socialness of being alone. I have tried to show that when we are acting all alone and seemingly in private, this does not mean that we are in a social-context vacuum. We can extend this to other things we do.

In hunting/gathering and agrarian societies, gaining resources came from cooperation within close groups, almost all of which were family- or kin-based, and it was clear that all behavior was related to the social relationships. Everything revolved around the family and community, and, as we have seen, being alone was problematic rather than a normal state of affairs. Many communities living within modernity are still structured in the same way.

It might be thought that modernity ushered in a new era in which our behavior was no longer determined to the same extent by social relationships, since most people we deal with are not closely involved in our affairs or related to us. However, this is very misleading, I believe. Relationships between strangers are certainly *different* from those among kin-based communities, but there are still strong relationships (albeit different ones) and our resources still very much come from those (stranger) relationships.

The relationship problem in modernity is that we are now dependent upon strangers for most of our resources but it is less clear what is required of us to maintain those relationships (compared to family cooperatives), and so much of our behavior now goes into maintaining reputations, personal image management, being up with the latest and the greatest, impressing people, keeping up on Facebook, knowing what we should know and a few things no one else does, showing off, and acting in ways that gain the attention of people who otherwise have no other (i.e. familial) interest in you. Because it is unclear what is even required of us to fulfill these goals, this means, in fact, that we might now spend *more effort* on social relationships than earlier forms of society, but in very different ways. This in turn means that we would have even *more* of our actions socially controlled but not in direct ways. Our behavior is therefore still socially controlled but through maintaining appearances and impressing people who are strangers, on the whole, not keeping onside with our families. This now takes up a large part of our time, energy, and money.

So the argument is that far from being freer of other people and more distant and independent, as modernity strengthens and as kin-based communities lose their influence, those 'in modernity' have probably become far *more* dependent on others, but dependent more upon whims and fads and fashions guiding the individual through multiple stranger relationships rather than the more direct or obvious resource implications found in closely structured families and communities. In terms of analysis, we must look for different sorts of social influences on everyday life, but social influences nonetheless. Different types of social influences now resonate as the contexts for acting, talking, and thinking.

What does the wave metaphor get us?

I wish to finish off this chapter by pointing out many cases for which the particle/causal metaphor has inhibited our understanding. We might appear to have a good understanding but that is because the 'causes' are put into abstract, non-observable, 'internal', non-interactive 'things' inside the body, so it really is not any sort of understanding at all – it is acquiescence in dogma.

The cases where the waves and the resonating guitar strings are of most value are the myriad examples of human behavior for which nothing is seen happening and yet people claim that there are powerful forces making them do something or preventing them from doing something. Many of these are the weirdest of human behaviors, and are rightly difficult to understand. Locking our understanding of these into mostly unknowable regions of the brain or 'psyche' is not helpful; describing the many contexts of those persons' lives will be more helpful.

One recent sad case that arose while I was writing this was that of an employee of a US Naval dockyard who took a gun to work and killed people. He had been claiming that he was being affected by electromagnetic waves that were pressuring him but no one understood him. The electromagnetic waves then pressured him to take revenge by killing people. Rather than focusing on the actual waves metaphor he used, we should see that what he was getting at was that there were powerful pressures in his life, pressures which had no obvious source or audience (or else he would have just said that his wife pressured him, for example), which could not be seen or remembered from any specific episodes (or he would have said it was triggered by a particular incident), but which were very real all the same (despite being invisible) and which strongly influenced him (despite seeming to come from nowhere).

The point is that for examples like this – and spirituality, hearing voices, psychoses, generalized anxiety, jinn, spirit possession, charisma, possession, intrusive thoughts, negative thoughts, bizarre thoughts, etc. – even if we do not believe there is anything more than material objects in this world, thinking in terms of people being influenced from their social contexts like sympathetically resonating guitar strings gives us far more understanding of these events and a sense of their reality than any of the particle/causal metaphors. We can also start to pin-point the audiences (past or generalized, usually, in these cases) for these behaviors and make contextual observations to describe those contexts as fully as social anthropologists. The same applies to many everyday behaviors, such as thoughts 'popping into your head' unexpectedly. Or imagine walking along a track and suddenly turning around, perhaps with the thought, "Oh, I forgot I have to see Mary today. Better get home quickly," even though there was no 'stimulus' (particle) for this in the environment. We will learn more about this once we deal with metaphors for language and thinking in the next two chapters.

The metaphor for now, however, is that our environment, apart from our interactions with objects and events, consists of a space (as if) filled with social waves resonating if we have the history or other attunement that is appropriate. We do not have to have an immediate 'trigger' around us, and these resonances are multiple and ongoing. This is how I think we should be metaphoring our social world of human behavior.

References

Azmitia, M., & Hesser, J. (1993). Why siblings are important agents of cognitive development: A comparison of siblings and peers. *Child Development*, 64, 430–444.

Bailey, F. G. (1991). *The prevalence of deceit*. Ithaca, NY: Cornell University Press.

Bakeman, R., & Adamson, L. B. (1984). Coordinating attention to people and objects in mother–infant and peer–infant interaction. *Child Development*, 55, 1278–1289.

Baldwin, D. A. (1993). Infants' ability to consult the speaker for clues to word references. *Journal of Child Language*, 20, 395–418.

Baldwin, D. A., & Markman, E. M. (1989). Establishing word–object relations: A first step. *Child Development*, 60, 381–398.

Bentley, A. F. (1935). *Behavior knowledge fact*. Bloomington, IN: Principia Press.

Bentley, A. F. (1941). The human skin: Philosophy's last line of defense. *Philosophy of Science*, 8, 1–19.

Berger, P. L., & Luckmann, T. (1967). *The social construction of reality: A treatise in the sociology of knowledge*. London: Penguin Books.

Billig, M. (2001). Humour and embarrassment: Limits of 'nice-guy' theories of social life. *Theory, Culture & Society*, 18, 23–43.

Billig, M. (2011). Writing social psychology: Fictional things and unpopulated texts. *British Journal of Social Psychology*, 50, 4–20.

Bloom, K. (1975). Social elicitation of infant vocal behavior. *Journal of Experimental Child Psychology*, 20, 51–58.

Bloom, K., Russell, A., & Wassenberg, K. (1987). Turn taking affects the quality of infant vocalizations. *Journal of Child Language*, 14, 211–227.

Brazelton, T. B., Koslowski, B., & Main, M. (1974). The origins of reciprocity: The early mother–infant interaction. In M. Lewis & L. A. Rosenblum (Eds.), *The effects of the infant on its caregiver* (pp. 49–76). New York: Wiley.

Burke, N. J., Joseph, G., Pasick, R. J., & Barker, J. C. (2010). Theorizing social context: Rethinking behavioral theory. *Health Education & Behavior*, 36, 55S–70S.

Butterworth, G., & Grover, L. (1988). The origins of referential communication in human infancy. In L. Weiskrantz (Ed.), *Thought without language* (pp. 5–24). Oxford: Clarendon Press.

Carugati, F., & Gilly, M. (1993). The multiple sides of the same tool: Cognitive development as a matter of social constructions and meanings. *European Journal of Psychology of Education*, 8, 345–354.

Cast, A. D., Stets, J. E., & Burke, P. J. (1999). Does the self conform to the views of others? *Social Psychology Quarterly*, 62, 68–82.

Clegg, B. (2012). *Gravity: Why what goes up, must come down*. London: Duckworth Overlook.

Cohen, A. (1971). The politics of ritual secrecy. *Man*, 6, 426–448.

Collis, G. M., & Shaffer, H. R. (1975). Synchronization of visual attention in mother–infant pairs. *Journal of Child Psychology and Psychiatry*, 16, 315–320.

Connor, D. B., Knight, D. K., & Cross, D. R. (1997). Mothers' and fathers' scaffolding of their 2-year-olds during problem-solving and literacy interactions. *British Journal of Developmental Psychology*, 15, 323–338.

Corkum, V., & Moore, C. (1998). The origins of joint visual attention in infants. *Developmental Psychology*, 34, 28–38.

Cox, B., & Forshaw, J. (2011). *The quantum universe: Everything that can happen does happen*. London: Penguin Books.

Deloria, V. (1994). *God is red: A native view of religion*. Golden, CO: Fulcrum Publishing.

Dennett, D. C. (1969). *Content and consciousness*. New York: Routledge.

Dewey, J., & Bentley, A. F. (1949). *Knowing and the known*. Boston: Beacon Press.

Doise, W., Mugny, G., & Perret-Clermont, A.-N. (1975). Social interaction and the development of cognitive operations. *European Journal of Social Psychology*, 5, 367–383.

Dunham, P. J., & Dunham, F. (1992). Lexical development during middle infancy: A mutually driven infant–caregiver process. *Developmental Psychology*, 28, 414–420.

Dunham, P. J., Dunham, F., & Curwin, A. (1993). Joint-attentional states and lexical acquisition at 18 months. *Developmental Psychology*, 29, 827–831.

Dunham, P. J., Dunham, F., Tran, S., & Aktar, N. (1991). The nonreciprocating robot: Effects on verbal discourse, social play, and social referencing at two years old. *Child Development*, 62, 1489–1502.

El Guindi, F. (1999). *Veil: Modesty, privacy and resistance*. New York: Berg.

Erickson, B. H. (1981). Secret societies and social structure. *Social Forces*, 60, 188–210.

Foucault, M. (1978). *The history of sexuality: Vol. 1. An introduction*. New York: Vintage Books.

Foucault, M. (1988). Technologies of the self. In L. H. Martin, H. Gutman, & P. H. Hutton (Eds.), *Technologies of the self* (pp. 16–49). London: Tavistock.

Franco, F., & Butterworth, G. (1996). Pointing and social awareness: Declaring and requesting in the second year. *Journal of Child Language*, 23, 307–336.

Gee, J. P. (1992). *The social mind: Language, ideology, and social practice*. New York: Bergin & Garvey.

Goffman, E. (1967). *Interaction ritual*. New York: Pantheon Books.

Görlich, J. (1998). Between war and peace: Gift exchange and commodity barter in the central and fringe highlands of Papua New Guinea. In T. Schweizer & D. R. White (Eds.), *Kinship, networks, and exchange* (pp. 303–331). New York: Cambridge University Press.

Guerin, B. (1993). *Social facilitation*. Cambridge, UK: Cambridge University Press.

Guerin, B. (2001). Replacing catharsis and uncertainty reduction theories with descriptions of the historical and social context. *Review of General Psychology*, 5, 44–61.

Guerin, B. (2004). *Handbook for analyzing the social strategies of everyday life*. Reno, NV: Context Press.

Hains, S. M. J., & Muir, D. W. (1996). Infant sensitivity to adult eye direction. *Child Development*, 67, 1940–1951.

Halle, T., & Shatz, M. (1994). Mothers' social regulatory language to young children in family settings. *First Language*, 14, 83–104.

Halliday, D., & Resnick, R. (1966). *Physics*. New York: John Wiley.

Hart, K. (1986). Heads or tails? Two sides of the coin. *Man*, 21, 637–656.

Herdt, G. (1990). Secret societies and secret collectives. *Oceania*, 60, 360–381.

Holland, R. (1977). *Self and social context*. London: Macmillan.

Innes, J. M. (1980). Fashions in social psychology. In R. Gilmour & S. Duck (Eds.), *The development of social psychology* (pp. 137–162). London: Academic Press.

Kantor, J. R., & Smith, N. W. (1975). *The science of psychology: An interbehavioral survey*. Chicago: Principia Press.

Karabenick, S. A. (1996). Social influences on meta-cognition: Effects of colearner questioning on comprehension monitoring. *Journal of Educational Psychology*, 88, 689–703.

Keen, I. (1994). *Knowledge and secrecy in an Aboriginal religion*. Oxford: Clarendon Press.

Kowalski, L., & Hellman, H. (1978). *Understanding physics*. Belmont, CA: Dickenson Publishing.

Landry, S. H., Garner, P. W., Swank, P. R., & Baldwin, C. D. (1996). Effects of maternal scaffolding during joint toy play with preterm and full-term infants. *Merrill-Palmer Quarterly*, 42, 177–199.

Lee, V. L. (1992). Transdermal interpretation of the subject matter of behavior analysis. *American Psychologist*, 47, 1337–1343.

Leung, E. H. L., & Rheingold, H. L. (1981). Development of pointing as a social gesture. *Developmental Psychology*, 17, 215–220.

Lewin, K. (1951). *Field theory in social science: Selected theoretical papers*. New York: Harper & Row.

Lodhi, S., & Greer, R. D. (1989). The speaker as listener. *Journal of the Experimental Analysis of Behavior*, 51, 353–360.

Manne, S. L. (1999). Intrusive thoughts and psychological distress among cancer patients: The role of spouse avoidance and criticism. *Journal of Consulting and Clinical Psychology*, 67, 539–546.

March, R. H. (1992). *Physics for poets*. London: McGraw-Hill.

Masur, E. F. (1982). Mothers' responses to infants' object-related gestures: Influences on lexical development. *Journal of Child Language*, 9, 23–30.

McCaffery, A. (1974). *The crystal singer*. London: Corgi Books.

McEvoy, J. P., & Zarate, O. (1999). *Introducing quantum theory*. London: Icon Books.

Mead, G. H. (1934). *Mind, self, and society from the standpoint of a social behaviorist*. Chicago: University of Chicago Press.

Merten, D. E. (1999). Enculturation into secrecy among junior high school girls. *Journal of Contemporary Ethnography*, 28, 107–137.

Messer, D. J. (1978). The integration of mothers' referential speech with joint play. *Child Development*, 49, 781–787.

Miller, P. J., Potts, R., Fung, H., Hoogstra, L., & Mintz, J. (1990). Narrative practices and the social construction of self in childhood. *American Ethnologist*, 17, 292–311.

Monteil, J.-M., & Huguet, P. (1999). *Social context and cognitive performance: Towards a social psychology of cognition*. London: Psychology Press.

Moore, C., Angelopoulos, M., & Bennett, P. (1997). The role of movement in the development of joint visual attention. *Infant Behavior and Development*, 20, 83–92.

Murphy, R. F. (1964). Social distance and the veil. *American Anthropologist*, 66, 1257–1274.

Newman, F., & Holzman, L. (1996). *Unscientific psychology: A cultural-performatory approach to understanding human life*. London: Praeger.

Nietzsche, F. (1967). *The will to power*. New York: Vintage Books.

Ninio, A., & Bruner, J. (1977). The achievement and antecedents of labelling. *Journal of Child Language*, 5, 1–15.

Papousek, M. (1995). Origins of reciprocity and mutuality in prelinguistic parent–infant 'dialogues.' In I. Marková, C. F. Graumann, & K. Foppa (Eds.), *Mutualities in dialogue* (pp. 58–81). Cambridge, UK: Cambridge University Press.

Peláez-Nogueras, M., Field, T., Gewirtz, J. L., Cigales, M., Gonzalez, A., Sanchez, A., & Richardson, S. C. (1997). The effects of systematic stroking versus tickling and poking on infant behavior. *Journal of Applied Developmental Psychology*, 18, 169–178.

Peláez-Nogueras, M., Gewirtz, J. L., Field, T., Cigales, M., Malphurs, J., Clasky, S., & Sanchez, A. (1996). Infants' preference for touch stimulation in face-to-face interactions. *Journal of Applied Developmental Psychology*, 17, 199–213.

Ratner, N., & Bruner, J. (1978). Games, social exchange and the acquisition of language. *Journal of Child Language*, 5, 391–401.

Read, J. G., & Bartkowski, J. P. (2000). To veil or not to veil? A case study of identity negotiation among Muslim women in Austin, Texas. *Gender & Society*, 14, 395–417.

Richardson, L. (1988). Secrecy and status: The social construction of forbidden relationships. *American Sociological Review*, 53, 209–219.

Riches, D. (1994). Shamanism: The key to religion. *Man*, 29, 381–405.

Roe, K. V., & Drivas, A. (1997). Reciprocity in mother–infant vocal interactions: Relationship to the quality of mothers' vocal stimulation. *American Journal of Orthopsychiatry*, 67, 645–649.

Rose, N. (1996). *Inventing our selves: Psychology, power, and personhood*. Cambridge, UK: Cambridge University Press.

Saxon, T. F., Frick, J. E., & Colombo, J. (1997). A longitudinal study of maternal interactional styles and infant visual attention. *Merrill-Palmer Quarterly*, 43, 48–66.

Schieffelin, E. L. (1976). *The sorrow and the lonely and the burning of the dancers*. Brisbane: University of Queensland Press.

Searle, J. R. (1995). *The construction of social reality*. New York: The Free Press.

Serway, R. A., Vuille, C., & Faughn, J. S. (2009). *College physics*. London: Brooks/Cole.

Simmel, G. (1950). *The sociology of Georg Simmel*. New York: The Free Press.

Simmel, G. (1907/1978). *The philosophy of money*. London: Routledge & Kegan Paul.

Skinner, B. F. (1957). *Verbal behavior*. Englewood Cliffs, NJ: Prentice Hall.

Smail, D. (2005). *Power, interest and psychology: Elements of a social materialist understanding of distress*. Ross-on-Wye: PCCS Books.

Smith, K. E., Landry, S. H., Miller-Loncar, C. L., & Swank, P. R. (1997). Characteristics that help mothers maintain their infants' focus of attention. *Journal of Applied Developmental Psychology*, 18, 587–601.

Taussig, M. (1987). *Shamanism, colonialism, and the wild man: A study in terror and healing*. Chicago: University of Chicago Press.

Tetlock, P. E., & Manstead, A. S. R. (1985). Impression management versus intrapsychic explanations in social psychology: A useful dichotomy? *Psychological Review*, 92, 59–77.

Thomas, N. (1992). Politicised values: The cultural dynamics of peripheral exchange. In C. Humphrey & S. Hugh-Jones (Eds.), *Barter, exchange and value: An anthropological approach* (pp. 21–41). New York: Cambridge University Press.

Tomasello, M., & Farrar, M. J. (1986). Joint attention and early language. *Child Development*, 57, 1454–1463.

Trevarthen, C. (1979). Communication and cooperation in early infancy: A description of primary intersubjectivity. In M. Bullowa (Ed.), *Before speech: The beginning of interpersonal communication* (pp. 321–347). London: Cambridge University Press.

Ugiris, I. C. (1991). The social context of infant imitation. In M. Lewis & S. Feinman (Eds.), *Social influences and socialization in infancy* (pp. 215–251). New York: Plenum.

Watson, A. C., Nixon, C. L., Wilson, A., & Capage, L. (1999). Social interaction skills and theory of mind in young children. *Developmental Psychology*, 35, 386–391.

Wertsch, J. V. (1985). *Vygotsky and the social formation of mind*. London: Harvard University Press.

Wertsch, J. V. (1991). *Voices of the mind: A sociocultural approach to mediated action*. London: Harvester Wheatsheaf.

Wittgenstein, L. (1958). *Philosophical investigations*. Oxford: Basil Blackwell.

Wood, D., Bruner, J. S., & Ross, G. (1976). The role of tutoring in problem solving. *Journal of Child Psychology and Psychiatry*, 17, 89–100.

Yngvesson, B., & Mahoney, M. A. (2000). 'As one should, ought and wants to be': Belonging and authenticity in identity narratives. *Theory, Culture & Society*, 17, 77–110.

3 Language use as the original virtual reality

In the previous chapter I argued that our behavior is socially controlled, even talking to yourself or thinking, as we will discover later. However, language is usually treated as mysterious and complex, as a process that bursts forth from within the person as if from an inner well of ideas. Some linguists 'explain' all this by an inner 'Language Acquisition Device' coupled to a cognitive processing system. There are all sorts of other metaphors along these lines that substitute as explanations for where language 'comes from'. My goal in this chapter is to suggest that once the causal/particle metaphors are gone, perhaps replaced by my wave metaphor and resonance, perhaps by something else, then most of what we think we know about language is wrong – plain and simple. I am not alone in this and there have been voices in the wilderness for decades trying to correct the main ideas about language, but the overarching beliefs about psychology (taken from common sense) once again have interfered with trying to think outside the box.

To try and get you thinking differently about language, in this chapter I will use the idea (not actually a metaphor!) that *language is the first and original virtual reality*. Some have tried this analogy before but without connecting the language to real-world social events and power (Ryan, 2001). What we really need are new ways to think about language use and have them lead to new ways to study and change language use.

Words do not control language use: social contexts do

The main ways in which language is thought about and talked about basically boil down to four:

- expression (words express something …)
- communication (words communicate something …)

- reference (words refer to something …)
- representation (words represent something …).

To me, these constitute the 'flat Earth' ideas about how language works – the ideas that seem perfectly sensible in everyday life, and indeed get us by in everyday life, but which fall apart when looked at closely. This is like the changes that came with the Theory of Relativity (Einstein, 1924/2007; Matthews, 2005), in that for everyday life we do not need to comprehend that we are gaining weight (or at least mass) when we move faster, or that when a dish falls in the kitchen and breaks that the gravity involved is really a warp or bend in the space-time fabric (Chown, 2007). A number of scholars have made one or two of these points about language separately (Bentley, 1935, 1941/1975; Cicourel, 1973; Gee, 1992; Harré, 1976; Mills, 1940; Potter, 2006; Sartwell, 2000; te Molder & Potter, 2005; Wertsch, 1985) but I want to bring them all together and ask you to repudiate these four common fallback explanations and instead substitute external social strategies and powers as the source of the language we use.

Unlike relativity, however, in the case of language I think that rethinking how language works actually helps us understand more about ourselves and our relationships to other people even in everyday life. It also makes sense of some paradoxes of language use, especially those to do with thinking and talking to yourself about yourself. For example, if scary stories, bizarre medical incidents, gory recollections, and horror themes are so aversive to people, why do people spend so much time telling them? Why do people spend so much time sitting around talking about banalities and repeating gossip and rumors that everyone already knows about? Are these a total waste of time in our lives or do they have some uses? Why do scientists invent jargon? Why do you bother listening to a friend tell a boring story when you would rather be somewhere else doing something else altogether?

To give you a heads-up as to where I am going, what has been missing from most accounts of language, and what I want to redress in this chapter, there are two initial questions:

- How is language able to make anything happen, how does it do anything, how does it affect the world?
- What exactly is the role of other people in making language work, how do our relationships become entwined in language use?

My first suggestions, for you to take initially on board in good faith as mantras to repeat even if you do not yet fully grasp them, are these:

- Avoid 'explaining' language uses by expression, communication, reference, and representation (except in everyday life).
- Think about language use in terms of *what it actually does*.
- For language to do anything many conditions need to be in place.
- These conditions that brings about speaking and writing are neither simple nor easy to observe (hence the wave and resonance metaphors will be useful).
- What language actually does (its consequences) is never simple nor easy to observe (and Holistic Elephant methodologies are very important).
- Following Chapter 2, be ready to see the *essential role of other people and social relationships in language use* even in the most intimate 'talking to oneself' (this will be addressed in Chapter 4).
- How we talk about things and events is not at all how they are.

When the Theory of Relativity was introduced in the early 1900s there were very few people in the world who could possibly comprehend what was being said and what the implications were; possibly only a dozen people. The ways of explaining relativity at that time were based only in complex mathematics and there were no easy anecdotes to give people the idea. Now, relativity is taught in early school levels and children can get the idea. Starting with Einstein himself, many ways to help understanding have been developed (Einstein, 1924/2007). Einstein developed the famous one of: "Imagine you are standing on a train going 100mph and you dropped something over the side. How would that look to someone standing motionless on the ground next to the train track and how would that look to someone traveling in a car driving at 60mph alongside the train?"

To rethink the uses of language we do not yet have a big set of such 'thought experiments' or anecdotes. In this chapter I want to start this by *comparing language use to the use of virtual reality technology*. This is nice because it shows how to put the social context back into explaining language use and shows how *social relationships rather than words or a language structure underpin the use of language*. It will help you (hopefully) with the hardest switch in thinking – to not focus on the 'meaning' of words that are said, but *to focus on what other people do when words are spoken*. In Chapter 4, I will look at the even trickier question: how can we also think about self-talk (thinking, cognition) as a social event involving other people – how can we contextualize thinking? That will be even harder to wrap your thinking around! It also changes how you observe the world and people around you, once again as 'contextual observation'. When someone says something you must spend the same, or, as I find, more time looking at how this is affecting the *listeners*, rather than focusing on the person *speaking*, and you need to know about the social relationships between speakers and listeners. But you also learn more that way.

Some of these points are raised by the people who write about the 'social construction' of knowledge, but I find they usually emphasize the 'construction' part rather than the 'social' part. Much of what is written is also about individual or cognitive 'social' construction that is not really social at all. But why would I go along with someone's construction? What is gained? What would I have to do to bolster or gain support for my social construction that I am the King of England – what social contexts would I have to put in place? These ideas can focus you better on the social basis of social constructionism: what are the limits on what I can socially construct? (answer: depends on the relationships with listeners); how does language make anything happen – how does it have consequences? (answer: through people).

In summary, there has been too much emphasis on the words as the main force of language – there has been too much focus on texts and 'intertexts' (Sartwell, 2000). But language itself is useless, and it can do nothing of consequence without other people. This is why Chapter 2 was important – we must refocus on *the consequences or power that allows language to have effects*, and that is precisely where the ubiquitous social context from the last chapter becomes overwhelmingly important.

Magic, words, and power

Most often words are reduced to some other frame, such as cognitive processes or stimulus-responses, and what seem to be 'special' or 'magic' words to us are reduced to something mechanical.

> I don't really do textual commentary. For me, a text is nothing but a cog in a larger extra-textual practice. It's not about using deconstruction, or any other textual practice, to do textual commentary; it's about seeing what one can do with an extra-textual practice that extends the text.
>
> (Deleuze, 2004, p. 260)

Looked at contextually, however, we can recapture the magic of words, but not 'inside' the words by themselves or 'inside' the persons. The words are not magic; as Deleuze puts it in the quotation above, the extra-textual practices or contexts are the magic. So if you have a special mantra to repeat, or some 'feel-good' words ("I am special"; "Today is the beginning of the rest of my life!"), the analysis is that the words themselves do not have a magical quality but the contexts around those words, what brought them into existence and what maintains their use now, are really the magic and these are very much real events. This will be social, as in saying the mantra is powerful because it allows you access into a whole realm of ways of life and strategizing with other people that would not be possible otherwise. So they can be very real but just in another way. As we will see, and this has enormous implications, just telling people what to do (e.g. "Stop smoking, it is harmful") provides no magic for people to do what you want. The social contexts and social relationships need to be arranged so they work; the words themselves are like mere props.

These arguments about language use relate to the very foundations of language being social. Words have an effect on the world only through other people (who have been trained in a certain way) and language use can therefore have consequences only through other people. All language use depends on other people, because using language does not do anything to the world, not even to language itself as part of the world. When the extent of language use in controlling human behavior is appreciated in this way, the scope of social control over 'individual' human behavior is greatly enlarged whether the person is alone or not. It does not even matter that the person is alone, as we saw at length in Chapter 2, and we can also now rethink social influence as like waves that resonate even at a distance. This argument will be made again for language use but in a different way through the virtual reality argument below.

The following is the main strong implication I would draw out from what has been said so far for trying to think about being alone as a social activity: *Language is something that only works or makes things happen with people involved.* If language is to 'work', to have a consequence, influence, or effect, then other people, relationships, outcomes, are required. Saying "Cat" only has an effect, and therefore consequences, through other people, not on any cat. This also applies to the speaker (Lohdi & Greer, 1989; Skinner, 1957). In this way, *words do not refer to things; they do things to people with an appropriate history* (Guerin, 1997). The ubiquity of language activities, even when one is alone, means that this point enlarges the scope of social control of human activity. The social becomes even more ubiquitous than it was shown to be in Chapter 2. To put it even more strongly: *Language use is more about influencing social relationships than it is about the words used or the things and events that seems to be referenced.*

Language use as the original virtual reality

If language has no effect on the environment except for other people or through other people, then we obviously need some new ways to be able to think this: to reimagine and rethink. This time, however, I am not providing a metaphor since I believe that it is within the scope of the term 'virtual reality'. So this is not a metaphor of language use, but language use was actually the original virtual reality. It was really the first virtual reality.

Metaphor 7. Language use as the original virtual reality

Having stated the broad outlines, I now want to provide a thought experiment to make this more real to readers. This will argue that whatever is meant by 'virtual realities', language was the first. Let me start with a version of a normal virtual reality machine, and go carefully through the steps involved. Then we will compare this to language use, and this will hopefully show you clearly the role of other people in all language use.

Suppose we have a hospital bed in a modern surgery. There is an open wound on a patient where we hope to do surgery but the surgery needs special microscopic implements. So we have a camera on the open wound and the image of this wound is digitized into a signal that is sent to another machine for the surgeon to look at. Note that this machine with the surgeon could be in the same room, in the next room, or on the other side of the world. (In fact, a probe that landed on Mars recently had equipment that was guided by someone on Earth in a similar way to what I am outlining here – someone looking at a screen on Earth could manipulate some tools that caused the same tools on Mars to move in the same way. The same applies to guidance systems for military drones. Anyway, we are getting ahead here too much, so back to the surgeon and the patient person on the table.)

To understand what follows it might help to look at some virtual surgery machines. I would urge you, if you are not squeamish, to look at some of these videos and sites, to see that this is concrete and real right now:

- https://www.youtube.com/watch?v=VJ_3GJNz4fg
- http://www.nycrobotic.com/advantages_of_robotic_surgery.php
- http://www.spacecoastlivinghealth.com/the-%E2%80%9Cnon-cutting%E2%80%9D-edge-of-advanced-surgery/
- http://itgs.wikispaces.com/Robotic+Surgery
- http://www.howstuffworks.com/robotic-surgery1.htm
- or if you are squeamish watch the videos on http://www.gwroboticsurgery.com/why-robotic-surgery.

The surgeon looks into a screen which can be like a television screen or a more digital version. What the surgeon sees could be the most realistic picture of the open wound or it could be contrast-enhanced or in some other way made more useful for the surgeon to work with. Just to emphasize this point, which will become important, *the signal coming from the camera does not need to be a perfect representation of the wound* or perfectly show the wound; we can also imagine a more high-tech version in which the digitized view of the wound (which is just computer data after all) is put through a filter which translates it into numbers corresponding to the morphology of the wound (like a digitized geographic version of a landscape showing lighter colors [or smaller numbers] where the land is higher and darker colors [or higher numbers] where the land is shallower). We could also send an infra-red version to the surgeon to manipulate, if seeing heat levels was somehow useful.

So what the surgeon operates with does not have to 'look like' the wound. In surgery a close resemblance is probably best, but in the case of language having a word resemble the referent would be unhelpful (the words 'cat' should not have to look like a cat).

Now once the surgeon has something to work with, they move their hands with gloves on, with handles, or with some other interface, which in turn moves a scalpel or another instrument hovering over the wound (I will stick with the gloves in what follows). They can then operate or stitch up the wound at a distance through looking at a 'virtual reality' of the wound with 'virtual' hands moving the (very real) instruments on the wound. I will come back to a fascinating addition to this in Chapter 4, when we will consider the surgeon looking at a wound on his or her own back and operating on his or her own back through a virtual picture and virtual hands. (That is one way we will tackle 'talking to yourself'.)

Now one point of this example is that there is nothing mysterious, magical, or extraterrestrial going on – this happens frequently around the world right now. Let us go over the steps to be clear, and to spell out the points I want to make. There is a person (surgeon) who is given a *fake* event to look at (the 'virtual' image or digitized enhancements). Through a lot of training, the surgeon then *responds to the fake rather than the reality*, and then through a second machine (in the present case) the surgeon's movements cause *real events* to occur in the original location (the wound). Another key point is that what the surgeon sees does not have to look like the reality, although for surgery you probably want this to be the case. But we can imagine virtual realities in which a person is represented as an avatar of their real body, nothing like the actual reality. We can also imagine cases in which what the surgeon thinks their hand movements are doing is not what is really happening at the other end (although again, this is probably not useful or safe for surgery). The point is that there does not have to be any resemblance if the purpose is fulfilled. If what is done at the other end is useful then we can imagine it being carried out. (For military drones a screen showing heat patterns or infra-red might actually be more useful than what you would see through your eyes or a regular camera on the drone.)

The other point to take away is that the linking of the gloves and the doctor's machine and the second (cutting) machine takes many years to develop. Any other machine would not work, or would produce ghastly results. If the glove machine and the cutting machine are not built (or *attuned* – see where I am heading with this?) in the same way then the results will also not occur. The glove machine will have no effect on anything if the machine with the precisely tuned blade is not there. Nothing will happen when the gloves are moved around.

So how does this pertain to language use? The question to keep in mind here is, "How does language do anything?" How does language make a difference in the world? In this way I want you to see that the second machine with the patient (the one that actually chops up the patient) in the case of language use is *other people*. When the surgeon manipulates the gloves (for language use that is equivalent to the surgeon speaking), the only effect those gloves have in the real world is to affect another machine (other people in the case of language) if they are tuned properly (if the other person has learned the language in the same way). The only effect or use of those glove movements is what is then done to the second machine and what that does to the world (chop up the patient or something). Doing the glove movements has no effect on anything else, no one else is saved or cured by those glove movements *unless* they are connected and tuned to the second machine. The gloves on the surgeon themselves are nowhere near the patient and really touch only thin air.

Now, the next thing to consider is what it is exactly that the other person does. In the case of surgery, the engineers have spent many years developing and refining the precise instrumentation on the second machine to operate correctly when the gloves are manipulated in certain ways. What about language, though? Two things that we tend to forget are: (1) we have all spent many years learning to respond to a language, and (2) the responses we have learned can be very complex and intricate – we spend a lot of our lives tuning ourselves to respond in certain ways when spoken to. As always, language seems to pop out of nowhere, as if we were born speaking (and many researchers have been misled into taking this seriously). But it takes, on average, about *15–20 years* to learn a language with most of the intricacies and nuances of context. And consider these amazing intricacies of language use (far superior I think to the virtual surgical-blade maneuvers!):

(1) John, if you could go downstairs and get my book, and turn to page 39 and bend the corner for me, then take it into the kitchen and put it on the blue shelf above the stove, I am sure we can come to some arrangement about what your punishment will be for hurting the cat.
(2) What you need to know is that the health system as a whole is guided by certain principles that pertain to events well beyond the physical health of patients. If it were only about bodily function then several layers of administration would be unnecessary.
(3) Two haiku:
People nowadays
don't want death because they'll miss
the next episode.

OMG I missed
2 pop-culture references.
My life is over!
(4) I once knew a man with one leg called Smith. Never found out what his other leg was called!
(5) One cat is up the tree. Many cats are up the tree.

Try teaching your dog to respond usefully to those! Each of these is relatively straightforward for those of us who have had 15–20 years learning English (and the same occurs in any language). But if you consider the complexities of what each of these is actually doing, you might begin to realize that our time at school was not wasted after all. They are pretty complicated. The first one, for example, is not very complex English but if we tried to teach that to a dog we would need many sessions. The last two are an example of something in a pattern that we do without thinking at all but which is a relatively complex pattern, especially if we tried to teach it to a dog. Many people cannot even describe the rule involved explicitly in (5) even though they can do it perfectly well. And as for the haiku: they do something to us but we hardly know what.

So I want you to be *amazed* at what we can do with language, even though in everyday life we fail to appreciate this. The surgeon's machine seems really fancy and impressive and high-tech, but *what we do with language is even more fancy and impressive*, although we must not forget that we have each spent a long time learning those intricacies, and tuning our own responses to each other.

So where we have got to in this? Basically, *the language we speak is a fake*. But not a fake in any mysterious sense, just a fake in the sense that the surgeon manipulates the gloves as if the gloves were touching the patient but they are actually a fake – the gloves do not even go near the patient's body and the surgeon is looking at a screen. But the glove manipulations still do cause the other machine to respond in ways that are hopefully useful, but not always. And with language, our words are fakes but they do cause other people to respond in ways that are hopefully useful, although not always. But *the gloves are useless without the other attuned machine, and our words are useless without other trained people there*. This is difficult to get a good gut feel for so I will illustrate more.

When we say "Look at the cat!" those words are a fake. The word 'cat' is not a cat. The word does not even look like a cat nor does the sound 'cat' sound at all like a cat. And the cat certainly does not respond when we say "Look at the cat!" *It is a sham!* But, the point is that with 15–20 years of similar training, it becomes a very useful sham because we can sometimes (not always, depends on the context) get people to behave in certain ways. So unless something sneaky is going on, when we say "Look at the cat!" a person is likely to look at the cat in the room. (By 'something sneaky' we could imagine that we are playing 'Simon says' and I did not say "Simon says look at the cat!" Or I have been bossing that person around so much that they no longer respond to my commands and are being oppositional. In terms of medical virtual realities this would be equivalent to turning the medical machine off at the wall or damaging the instruments so they would not work in the trained way either. Or something I do not want to think about – the second machine malfunctioning in the middle of an operation ...)

When you hear and read what I am saying above, it commonly seems just so obvious, but this does not come through in everyday life and in theories of language. We usually just say in a shorthand way that our words 'mean' for us to look at the cat, which does not help us. But

Table 3.1 Comparison of language use and medical virtual reality machines

Virtual reality medical machines	*Language use*
The glove machine can do nothing by itself	Talking out loud does nothing to the world by itself
The two machines need to be carefully tuned to each other for anything to happen	The two speakers need to be trained in the same language use
Developing and tuning the machines takes a lot of time	We take a long time to learn a language properly
The only effect of the glove machine is to affect the second machine, it does nothing to the patient	The only effect of speaking is to do something to other people; speaking does not affect anything else in the world, even the 'referent'
Only the second machine does anything to the world	Only the second speaker (listener) does anything directly to the world when we speak
The gloves do not touch the patient	Saying 'Cat' does not affect any cat; to touch a map is not to touch the ground
What the surgeon sees does not have to exactly reflect the actual wound	Our words do not have to represent or mimic what the speaker will do upon hearing them (except rare onomatopoeia)
The effects of the gloves are not always the same or exact, especially if two different 'second' machines are used	Our words do not always have the same effects on people, especially different people and in different contexts
For the gloves to have closely repeatable effects the tuning between machines must be precise	To have the same effects of words on different people or the same person twice, there must be very exact training of language use and strong outcomes from doing what was trained
The meaning or effect of the gloves is what the second machine does, not what is seen on the screen (represented or referenced on the screen)	The meaning of words is whatever other people do in the world when listening, not what is supposedly represented, communicated, expressed, or referenced
The 'definition' of what a glove movement does is defined by what the second machine does and how precisely they are tuned	The definition of words depends on how precise the training has been and the social contexts for other people following the training
The second machine does not have to be in the same room or country as the surgeon and the glove machine	The listener does not have to be present (we can use our mobile)
The image on the screen can be enhanced or changed depending on what is useful; it is a fake in any case	The words can be changed in any way to get different effects: "Feed the cat!", "Can you please feed the little white fluffy kitten in the lounge room?" They are a fake in any case and only what the other person does is real (which depends in turn on their training)

I want you to get a good feel for this sequence of events. Academics also spend their whole time focusing on understanding the gloves rather than the role of the second machine. Table 3.1 can hopefully help you understand and remember all the points made.

In this way, I think about language use as the original virtual reality. We do something that bears no resemblance to what gets done, but because of a precisely trained second machine (attuned to resonate in a trained way even at a distance) things get done out there in the world (by the listener). We then need to learn to teach language use so that we can get more or less specific things done. Training the listener to use questions as their response helps with this problem in everyday life:

"Can you bring me the spoon on the ledge?"

"What, the silver one just below the pot plant?"

"Yes, thanks."

We can even imagine a sophisticated second machine in surgery that questions when the surgeon might be doing something wrong: "Surgeon-person, are you sure you want to cut right there? My sensors detect a jugular."

Now we get to even trickier thoughts. You can start to get a new mantra for this: that *other people are always involved in any and all language use*. Language is not something that spills out from within my 'inner self' (except as a metaphor for our long history and training that we commonly forget about – remember the Plasticine!), but whenever someone says something, other people are, or have been, involved. In Chapter 4, I will even apply this to cases when you might be *talking to yourself*, as we say, or thinking.

This means, in turn, another conceptually difficult mantra for most people: when you are talking, even talking to yourself, we always need to ask these questions:

- Who is the audience for this talk?
- Who has been an audience for this talk in the past?
- Is there a specific audience or a general audience?
- What responses might people be trained to respond with after hearing this talk?
- How specific is that training or should we expect a lot of variations?

These are questions that some psychotherapists actually use to help people with their 'private' chatter (Carey, 2008; Hayes, Strosahl, & Wilson, 2012; Perls, 1969). It must be kept clearly in mind, however, that the obvious response to something said is not always the useful one, in the way that 'Simon says' illustrated above. As another example, depending upon the current social strategies playing out in context,

I might actually be saying "Look at the cat!" so that the listener does *not* look out the window at that moment when something sneaky is going on. I do not really want them to see the cat; I actually just want them to look away from the window and be distracted! This is also why 'explaining' "Look at the cat!" as *meaning*, *expressing*, *representing*, or *communicating* that you want the listener to look at the cat is a poor social analysis – lots of other scenarios can actually be imagined, even ones that are the opposite of what seems to be meant. *Our analysis of social relationships and social strategies must come ahead of our analysis of the words used.*

Further, there is not always a specific outcome that is the useful one anyway: "Who can think of something that would help prevent people from looking at cats?" While I could have one specific answer 'in mind' (from my history), I might also be trying to brainstorm new ideas. And when the teacher says "Rome was founded on the back of a dying civilization that had run its course" there is no single, specific response – there are many, and some of those might be useful in context. But this is no different from saying that a hammer was designed to hit in nails and while it is usually used for that, it also gets frequently used for other activities not as precise, or saying that sometimes you use it but you miss. And we could use the virtual reality surgical machine for other, nefarious purposes (the plot for a new *Saw* movie?).

Two of the strangest and least examined implications of this view of language use are that:

- we cannot analyze language use by just analyzing the words that are used;
- we can only analyze language use within a social contextual analysis and with knowledge about the people involved and their relationship history.

Even if there are strangers talking with no history, this must be part of our analysis of what is going on and the social strategies being employed. For example, talking to strangers often produces responses we do not expect (sometimes this is good for psychotherapy). So the point is that *language analysis must be a social analysis* in all cases. You cannot study any language use just by considering the words – you must include the people involved and their relationship and history. It would be like trying to understand how the surgeon on the first machine can fix the patient without studying the second machine in the other room, especially if we cannot easily see it (reflecting the social contexts for language use we saw in Chapter 2).

Now for everyday life, once again we just assume that when we say "Look at the cat!" people will look at the cat (except for some trouble-makers with an oppositional attitude problem) and that when we say "Did you know that Lima is the capital of Peru?" the next day most people will remember that. These ways of talking are harmless, even if misleading from the new perspective, just as believing that the Earth is flat or that our mass remains the same when we move faster is harmless in everyday life. But, of course, it is also common for health professionals to assume that by saying "Cigarettes cause cancer so you must stop smoking" people will listen and respond by giving up cigarettes – but they do not. So in everyday life we mostly get by with assuming that language typically works like a flat Earth does, except for some problem cases.

Two metaphors that help rethink language use as virtual reality

The idea of language use as a virtual reality can help you weave your ways though the practical and philosophical problems when thinking about language. Chapter 5 pulls this together and looks more at the philosophical questions. I believe it is important to really (over)emphasize the messages coming from this idea because those messages go against our common ways of talking. So to help in this I will spend the rest of this chapter revisiting one old metaphor from the last chapter and then introducing a new one.

Back to electromagnetic waves

If you remember back to Chapter 2, I urged that our external contexts influence and control our actions, talk, and thinking, and to help think this I used the metaphor of waves rather than particles – likening this to the physicists' change of thinking in the early twentieth century from particle to wave thinking. We can now wonder how that wave metaphor looks when we are thinking about language use specifically. In the next chapter we will get to how we can think about thinking as waves.

Metaphor 8. Language better thought of as attuned responses to waves than as reactions to particles

Here I want to revisit an old metaphor to help you rethink how external contexts bring about our language use, and especially the social context. Once again I am not suggesting a theory that external contexts affect us by emitting electromagnetic waves into our brains, or anything science-fictionish like that. Rather, the whole process of electromagnetic waves is puzzling in real life and yet during the late nineteenth century and early twentieth century physicists had a major rethink and by changing some preconceived ideas they rethought many physical phenomena. They have not got all the answers yet, but that is also part of my point. I am merely utilizing the physicists' major change from thinking in terms of particles and causes to thinking in terms of waves and context.

We wander around the world talking to people when we meet, and sometimes it seems we just blurt things out but at other times it seems as if we control what we say and can point to strategies in what we say. When we are asked about our talk we therefore (*contra* Chapter 1) think in terms of what in the immediate situation caused the talk. When there seems to be nothing obvious we can 'see' then we posit the usual 'inner' causes: "I must have been trying to provoke them, I guess!"

With my wave metaphor we can now imagine that there are also many not-present contexts controlling whatever we might say as we move around the world. The talk just 'pops out of our mouths', but this comes from a wide variety of our contexts influencing our behavior as resonance at a distance – temporal or spatial – not as particle-like causes from the immediate context. This has the strange (for everyday explanations, that is) implication that we will not know why we say half the things we say. It has the stranger implication also that someone studying all of our life contexts and situations might be in a better position to understand why we say the things we do than we do ourselves! Luckily, we rarely get people studying us this intently.

In everyday life the obvious context for talking is another person with us, but that is not necessary (see next chapter), nor when we talk to someone are we exclusively talking to them. We can talk to other people through the listener.

"It either happens or it doesn't": contexts are 100 percent

I do not wish to overburden you or freak you out with so many metaphors, but, at the risk of you giving up in despair, I want to introduce one last metaphor for Chapter 3. This brings together a point made a few times so far, but a point I did not pause to discuss. The messages and the changes in thinking about people that are entailed from the change to thinking about language use in this chapter are so far-reaching that I want to make sure you have different ways to get a gut feel for those entailments.

This new metaphor is to help you overcome a conundrum that often holds people up – they get stuck on it and cannot think any further. My solution is that both sides of the conundrum are rescued so you can move on. To help counteract this I have a sort-of-metaphor – "*What is real?*" *equals what in this situation will hit you like a brick?*

The problem starts because I have argued and 'metaphored' above to get you thinking about language use as being externally controlled through other people (they are metaphorically equivalent to the second virtual reality machines that do the cutting). There is an intellectual history (usually not a common-sense one) that things and events only exist if we think they do or if we want them to. Some of these views are just plain weird and New Age-ish, but others have something important to tell us. So for example, the social constructionists are obviously not talking total rubbish and have important things to affect our thinking (Searle, 1995), even though some cultural relativism arguments go overboard, I believe (e.g. Rosaldo, 1989). Likewise, people take courage in the statement of W. I. Thomas: "If men define situations as real, they are real in their consequences" (this, by the way, was actually jointly authored with his research assistant and future wife Dorothy Thomas in 1928, pp. 571–572).

Goffman, on the other hand, argued against extreme social constructionisms:

> There is a venerable tradition in philosophy that argues that what the reader assumes to be real is but a shadow, and that by attending to what the writer says about perception, thought, the brain, language, culture, a new methodology, or novel social forces, the veil can be lifted .... A current example of this tradition can be found in some of the doctrines of social psychology and the W. I. Thomas dictum: "If men define situations as real, they are real in their consequences." This statement is true as it reads but false as it is taken. Defining situations as real certainly has consequences, but these may contribute very marginally to the events in progress.
>
> (Goffman, 1974, p. 1)

A more assertive method is sometimes used in Zen training, as Reps illustrates:

> Yamaoka Tesshu, as a young student of Zen, visited one master after another. He called upon Dokuon of Shokoku.
>
> Desiring to show his attainment, he said: "The mind, Buddha, and sentient beings, after all, do not exist. The true nature of phenomena is emptiness. There is no realization, no delusion, no sage, no mediocrity. There is no giving and nothing to be received."
>
> Dokuon, who was smoking quietly, said nothing. Suddenly he whacked Yamaoka with his bamboo pipe. This made the youth quite angry.
>
> "If nothing exists," inquired Dokuon, "where did this anger come from?"
>
> (Reps, 1957, p. 75)

We cannot, however, discard the social constructionist thinking and pretend that it is just pure make-believe, but Marx, Goffman, Zen, and others are not wrong that there is also a non-negotiable world we cannot just verbalize away. But we need to find out what the force of words is, and where this force comes from, since I have argued that there is no inherent force living inside words. These quotations are certainly correct that, contrary to common sense, the force of words does not come from the words themselves. So to help guide this, I wish to present another metaphor and then see how we can get out of this conundrum. Chapter 5 will then bring all these pieces together, hopefully.

Metaphor 9. Getting hit 100 percent by a brick and other brute facts of life

I want to introduce a version of the 'brute facts' argument to judge reality (Anscombe, 1958). This seems simple for non-language events in our contexts, but it is when we get to language use that it becomes all murky ("Unicorns must exist in some sense if I can talk about them"). This metaphor applies to material in Chapters 1 and 2, but it is really crucial when rethinking language use, which is why it is here rather than in Chapter 1. This looks simple but it is not, so read carefully and a few times.

To start, I want you to consider the following: "But what about if a large brick fell on you, that would hurt, wouldn't it?"; "What about getting hit by a wall of bricks falling on you, surely that's not culturally relative?"; and, "But what if I hit you with a brick. Is *that* only socially constructed and relative?" The argument is that you cannot deny or be uncertain about these events – they are brute events in life – and so they are used to stand as counter-examples to the everything-is-relative and everything-is-socially-constructed arguments.

One tack to counter this in turn is to claim that we cannot actually be certain about the brick incident, either. It might have just been a dream. But this argument is one of the confusing perceptual errors with metaphysical doubts; longer and better observations would clarify, if we follow our *Metaphor of the Holistic Elephants*. Put graphically, by the time I hit you for the fifth time with a brick, you would have little of either perceptual or metaphysical doubt left. You would not care what Descartes or W. I. Thomas said. Redefining or socially constructing a reframing of being hit by a brick as 'a rather pleasurable sensation' would have gone out of the window!

This rethink can be extended in an interesting way, however, because if I were to repeat to you fifteen times, "This is a unicorn not a dog," "This is a unicorn not a dog," etc., you would ***not*** get that extra sense of certainty that hitting with bricks gives upon repetition. Think about that for a while. In fact, we begin to doubt a speaker even more if they say something repeatedly. It is perhaps cases like this that make people believe that *words cannot have any certainty*, or that *words have no brute events*, because repetition fails to convince or give certainty, under normal circumstances, compared to the way being repeatedly hit by a brick strongly convinces us of brute facts and that W. I. Thomas cannot help us.

But it is also these sorts of cases that give a clue as to our next question: *Just what* are *the brute events of language use?* I want to argue that language use does have brute events, just not in the way that 350 years of Descartes and 150 years of psychology have been thinking about it. That has been our problem. Just because saying "Unicorn" does not have a verifiable, certain, brute referent, does not mean it is bereft of brute events that impose reality on us. In fact, Western philosophy has been long misguided because it has been wrongly searching for the brute events of words in referents, expressions, communications, and representations.

The hitting with a brick is clearly doing something (within the limits of perceptual errors); it is having an effect on the world, a pragmatic effect if you like, and on the person being hit in particular. But what effects are the repeated words having? What is being done in the world when we say words? Correspondence theories in fact could be taken to imply that repetition should enforce or reinforce correspondence between the word and the thing, so repetition gives us the feel of real brute events. Indeed, some associationist positions implicitly contain this – Thorndike would have said that the repetition should 'stamp in' the association even harder and more brutally, whereas I suggested above that repeating "This is a unicorn not a dog," "This is a unicorn not a dog," etc., possibly makes it seem *less certain* to be a real unicorn, not more certain. I would begin to suspect the speaker's motives, as we say, or that "The lady doth protest too much, methinks," as Shakespeare wrote (and therein lies the clue for the astute reader!).

To get out of this conundrum of our metaphor of the brick, we simply go back to the virtual reality metaphor message:

(1) Words have no certain or brute correspondence to their traditional 'referents'.
(2) Words are only social in their effects. They have no effects (let alone correspondence) on the traditional 'referents' of sentences.
(3) Words only have effects on the listeners.

The current metaphor then, really poses this question: *For judging reality, where is your brick coming from?* Armed now with our virtual reality metaphor we can see that *the bricks from language use will only come from other people*. If we say "You are a stupid, stupid cat!" the cat does nothing (maybe proving the point, or the opposite?). But the loving owner of that cat might well throw a brick at you for insulting their cat!

The upshot is that we can know the 'real' world 100 percent within perceptual errors (holistic elephants), but the reality of words that are spoken is 0 percent – *Whatever is said is never real with respect to what we call expression, communication, representation, or referent*. The way out of this conundrum, which also allows us to keep the best of social constructionism, is that language use is still 100 percent real but the brute reality (where do the bricks come flying from?) is in *whatever people do when you say something*, not from reference or representation.

More will be drawn out from this in Chapter 5, especially after considering thoughts and thinking in the same way in the next chapter. This also solves a lot of Western philosophical problems of metaphysics as well, which is a bonus (Chapter 5). An appendix to this book gives an outline of the more formal philosophy for interested readers.

What does all this mean for language use?

Language use is the original virtual reality. So what? This view means several things coming from a 180° shift from what we normally think. Drawing on some earlier metaphors, the idea is that language arises as a specialized behavior that is only for interaction with people (this is certainly not new, however!). More specifically, and a bit more originally (Guerin, 1997), language is only there because it does things to people. The people do not have to be actually present, as seen in our electromagnetic waves metaphor, and the whole learning and maintenance of language as a life strategy is only possible through other people who have scaffolded it jointly along the way with us with intensive language training (Chapter 2).

Our two main tasks for language, then, are to analyze what it does exactly to people (and the speaker), and to find out the contexts in which these occur. Language use is part of other contextual strategies and does not have to immediately gain us some resources. For example, a lot of what we say is meaningless drivel and social chatter but has the extremely important resource function of keeping us in relationships with people. Having an active network of friends and family is probably the most important life strategy for gaining access to the resources we need. This means you do not want to waste time analyzing the 'meaning' of social chit-chat since it is part of a functioning context to strategize resources through social relationships. What is actually said can be pretty weird and meaningless. But in line with recent discourse and conversational analysis, and other viewpoints, you need to focus on the strategic functioning of language in social relationships. The brute events (the reality) of language use lie in what people do when you talk, even if it is not what you wanted.

The problem is that most recent forms of sociolinguistic and discursive analysis do not blend a thorough social analysis in with the language use analyses. *We need to find better ways to integrate 'linguistic' and social analyses* (Guerin, forthcoming). Another problem is that some of these language use analyses do not make the next 180° shift from what we normally think, and apply this equally to talking to ourselves or thinking. We will approach that in the next chapter.

So we need to focus on:

- What does language use do to people?
- What does it do to the speaker?
- How this is structured through the social relationships, social strategies and other contexts rather than the words *per se*.

Linguists are especially notorious for spending too much time making up categorizations of words rather than examining social relationships and other contexts in which those words are learned and then function (Guerin, 2003, 2004).

For example, if I say "Oh, look at that cat!", then we really cannot understand what is going on without knowing more about the relationships with the audience and other people who might be relevant but not present, the contexts from which the speech emerged, the social strategies going on and their histories, etc. This might not even involve a cat: it might involve me trying to look like a nice, caring, pet-loving sort of guy; it might involve a strategy to distract; it might be a game of 'Simon says'. Until we do those social analyses we will not know whether saying "Oh, look at that cat!" is part of a strategy to:

- try and be interesting to those present (perhaps be entertaining, if the cat is doing something noteworthy);
- try and get people to believe you are a gentle cat lover;
- try and get people to look in the direction of the cat so they do not see something else going on in another direction;
- an attempt to win 'Simon says';
- try and show off your language skills;
- try and irk someone who does not like cats;
- try and focus the talk on cats so you can tell a favorite story;
- etc.

We will never know the answers to this from the words alone. There are many possibilities and we need some social analysis to narrow these possibilities down. This is similar to any social analysis of possibilities, but we are looking in this chapter at only those strategies that involve language use. Even with just a smile there are many possibilities and some involve language strategies. Here is an example in which the one person smiles at another, but language use strategies might still be involved.

> "In a lecture class I see you smile at another student across the room."

What are some different types of social contexts that might bring about this sort of smiling in this context?

(1) You like that person or want to like them.
(2) You do not want that person to think you are ignoring them.
(3) You want to like someone they know who is not present right now.

(4) You like the group they belong to and want part of it.
(5) You want to borrow some money (more specific).
(6) You are avoiding looking the other way.
(7) You had a bet that you would smile at them.
(8) You have been to the dentist and your smile is fixed.
(9) You want someone to see you smile at them (to make them jealous?).
(10) You want to give the impression that you know people and have friends when you do not (reputation is the 'resource').
(11) You want to be able to tell someone afterwards that you smiled.

You might use language use strategies and not just a smile on possibilities (1), (3), (4), and (5), whereas the person here does not. For example, on possibility (3), you might smile and add, "Is Cathy here today? She has been missing and I worry when she is not here. Perhaps one of us should check on her? I could do it after class." But notice possibility (11). You might do things in many situations for which nothing in that present context is of interest (resources) to you, but what is of interest is that you can talk about it to significant others in your life (probably) afterwards. So you might tell your mates after lectures, "Wow. I smiled at that girl in the blue top today, and she smiled back a huge smile like she was really interested in me! I might ask her out soon." Perhaps total exaggeration with a dash of fiction, but if it works to impress your mates, who cares! The smiling was not about the girl so much as talking to your mates about it afterwards.

Another consequence of this 180° shift from what we normally think relates to Western philosophy, and metaphysics in particular. Since Descartes, most of the discussions around language and metaphysics have been about how language use (statements, propositions) can be true, whether words can be true when they express, represent, refer to, or communicate whatever it is they are supposed to. A lot of philosophers' time has been spent of reference: how can we believe that "That is a cat" is true? How do we know if it is true?

While more will be said of this fruitless quest (e.g. Deleuze, 1953; Quine, 1968) in Chapter 5, it can be seen how the virtual reality comparison makes a mockery of this. When I say "That is a cat" the language use is functioning with listeners and later audiences, the words are not representing or referring to anything. As expressed elsewhere, *words do not do anything to things; they can get listeners to do things if the training is there*. Or, *words have no effect on things; they only have effects on listeners*. Or for the latest point, *words do not refer to things; but they can refer other people to things*.

This can also be seen clearly, perhaps, when considering definitions of words. For a word to be precisely and exactly defined it is a matter of *gaining complete control over a listener*, not getting the words right. The more we can shape a person so that they do one thing and precisely only one thing when they hear a word, the more we can clearly define a word. However, given that we do not have such social control over people, very highly precise definitions are not going to be possible. A precise definition requires a replicable and precise effect on a listener, and whether or not that is possible depends upon the whims of socialization and social control.

So while in everyday life there obviously seems to be a correspondence between words and things, the present arguments suggest that *correspondence is a matter of training and history* rather than metaphysics (cf. Modée, 2000; Quine, 1974). If we designate 'looking at something' or 'pointing to something' as 'correctly corresponding' responses for a moment, then a sentence might be said to be true to the extent that the words correspond to the thing; that is, that a listener can reliably point to a blue dog when I say "That is a blue dog." But notice that this is a matter of training in three ways: in how well the listener has been taught the same language; in how closely we agree that pointing or looking at is the 'correct' answer; and in what outcomes for the listener there are if they do what they were trained to do. The correspondence is entirely contingent upon a training regime. Moreover, from the virtual reality argument, I could say "That is a blue dog" as part of a social strategy totally unrelated to any dog present, blue or otherwise. In all, there are also changes in how metaphysics and Western philosophy of knowledge is handled, but I will not say more here of that. Expect more, however, in Chapter 5.

I will make one last point that is entailed by all these metaphors and changes in thinking about language use. If we locate the brute reality of language use in the effects on other people and the consequences to us ("Where are the bricks coming from?"), then there are a range of things spoken about that will be socially constructed. That is, the *only* bricks coming back at us are from people who hear what we say and are trained appropriately; the rest of the universe remains steadfast and 'not amused'. Amongst these, I include:

- causality
- probability
- negation
- unicorns
- time

- contradiction.

Let me just talk about two of these that are of interest in the next chapter on thinking. I have already talked about causality in Chapter 1 and you could perhaps go back and see how this present discussion fits in there.

Probability and *negation* are interesting because when we separate ‘events and objects’ clearly from the ‘talking about events and objects’, in the way done here with our metaphors, then probability and negation cannot exist in the real brute world. In the world there are only 100 percent certain positives (within perceptual errors of observation, but remember the holistic elephant!). Sitting here next to me on my chair there is not ‘an absence of a watermelon’, even though there is no watermelon here. The absence of a watermelon can only come back at me like a brick if I talk about it with someone – *it is a talking event not a brick event in itself.* The case of ‘thinking about a watermelon next to me’ is tricky, but to give a heads-up, we will see in the next chapter that thinking is still dependent on other people (the surgeon operating on their own back still needs the second machine to be working, in our hospital comparison). And the person I tell about my absent watermelon friend might have me locked up for public safety – a very real brute event in my life.

In a similar way for probability, there is not a 50 percent chance of a watermelon being next to me. There is either a watermelon or there is not, and that again is a talking event and therefore needs another person (if we leave thinking about likelihood of watermelons appearing until the next chapter) before consequences (bricks) can occur. The ‘watermelon’ *not* being there is likewise purely a talking event. (For astute readers, I believe Schrödinger’s cat argument makes some of these same errors in reasoning, but enough of physics.)

This all means that you need to be thinking that for the contexts in which we live, everything is 100 percent real excepting for when we get perceptual and other errors. If we follow the metaphor and methodologies of the holistic elephant we should be able to reduce these. This is all very similar to the message of J. J. Gibson (1979) for perception – perception is an active doing thing that is 100 percent, but most experiments set up error-prone environments for testing (like visual illusions). He also included that we do not see things but we ‘see’ what the environment ‘affords’ rather than objects per se (very much like what I have called ‘contextual observation’).

A final point about *negation*. My point here is that there is no real brute negation; negation is only something that can be spoken about so its consequences will only come from listeners or readers, not from the world. A number of people have noted that in some contexts people do, in fact, stop referring to negations. For example, Sigmund Freud (e.g. 1910/1925) was interested in this because when he documented what for him was the 'unconscious', in dreams for example, he noted that there were no negatives:

> The attitude of dreams towards the category of antithesis and contradiction is most striking. This category is simply ignored; the word "No" does not seem to exist for a dream.
>
> (Freud 1910/1925, p. 184)

> There are in this system (unconscious, *Ucs*) no negation, no doubt, no degrees of certainty: all this is only introduced by the work of the censorship between *Ucs* and the *Pcs.* Negation is a substitute, at a higher level, for repression. In the *Ucs* there are only contents.
>
> (Freud, 1915/1984, p. 190)

A comparison of this will have to wait until Chapter 4 but this is saying, in present terms, that the real contexts (the unconscious is the world out there, not something in our head, it will turn out) are all 100 percent, and only in the preparing and rehearsing to talk and in actually talking to people (= preconscious, Pcs) does negation slip in and become invented. Moreover, Freud links this to the talking activities or strategies of wanting to disguise, hide, or repress some of those 100 percent things and events and so it negates them in words. But this does not mean that we can ignore negations as of no importance: there are still real consequences from negation, but they come from people (e.g. "You have no brains in your head whatsoever, and you lack all imagination, you idiot!").

As a practical method, if trying to get people to talk about these 100 percent events and things that have been negated, he recommended that when a person is reporting their associations or dreams, if they say a negative, treat the case as if that were actually the case and ignore the negatives.

> The manner in which our patients bring forward their associations during the work of analysis gives us an opportunity for making some interesting observations. "Now you'll think I mean to say something insulting, but really I've no such intention." We realize that this is a repudiation, by projection, of an idea that has just

> come up. Or: "You ask who this person in the dream can be. It's not my mother." We emend this to: "So it is his mother." In our interpretation, we take the liberty of disregarding the negation and of picking out the subject-matter alone of the association. It is as if the patient had said: "It's true that my mother came into my mind as I thought of this person, but I don't feel inclined to let the association count."
>
> (Freud, 1925/1984, p. 437)

We will examine this again after rethinking thoughts and thinking in the next chapter.

How does this affect the analysis of language use?

The question now is how does this rethinking about language as a virtual reality affect our everyday understanding of what people say and when they say it? There are a number of ways things change. First, the analyses of language use will turn out to be very different to linguistic analyses even while incorporating the latter. Linguistic analysis focuses on the structures of historically constructed languages used in conversations, but our language analysis will focus on what language use does socially – that is, what does language actually do to people; what can I do with language to other people?

Language use therefore is seen as just a way of influencing people to do all the sorts of things needed in living a life with cooperation from others. To put a nail in the wall we can use a rock and bang it in. We might better use a hammer merely because it is designed in a better way for banging in nails, and is less messy. Another way, though, would be to ask someone to nail it in the wall. How we do this, and whether it is successful, depends on all the things in our contexts, and especially the social relationships between you and the person asked to do the nail. It requires a social analysis linked with a linguistic analysis.

If you think about language use this way, it will help you in your analyses. Try and forget all the old notions of language as something which expresses, communicates, refers to, means, or represents. They will mess you up. Of most importance to notice at this stage, the virtual reality argument is meant to reinforce that *language use only has any effect in the world if it affects a person. By itself, without people, language can do nothing*.

What this means is that any analyses involving language must include the past or present audiences or populations (listeners sometimes) and what they do upon hearing the language used (even if it is not what is expected).

You cannot analyze language use without analyzing the audiences and relationships and the history of relationships and outcomes involved.

A lot of the material to help do this comes from discursive and conversational analysis research, which includes a lot of social strategizing in the analysis. However, much of that work does not *fully* analyze the social relationships and exchanges (what is done when hearing something said by someone) and usually there is a simple analysis or often a guess, even though the language/word side of things is analyzed in great detail. The language analysis might be detailed and useful, but the preamble social analyses do not usually have enough documentation of the contexts for us to really understand what the language strategies are doing in the relationship. Too much is taken for granted and assumed.

So language use is just an extension of any other strategy we might use, but a very useful one that has some fascinating properties. But it only works to do things to people it does not do anything to what it purports to describe. Saying "The cat is on the mat" can affect a person but not a cat; saying "Can you please hammer that nail into the wall for me" can affect a person but does not affect the nail or the wall (except indirectly through the person asked, if they oblige because of the relationship and history).

The future goal, then, is to merge the wonderful linguistics and discursive and conversational analyses with much more of the social analyses.

What do we need to know about language-in-social-interaction to understand people?

This book is not the place to outline discourse and conversational analysis in this way (Guerin, 2003, 2004, forthcoming). But there are many places in this chapter that change how we do that. I have already pointed out that more social analysis needs to be done in conjunction with discursive analysis, even though in principle it seems to be included. The *ubiquitous*, *virtual*, and *social* properties of language use require this.

The other major change to our everyday thinking about language use is from situating the locus of language use externally rather than from some inner locus that emits language. With the *external*, *virtual*, and *social* properties of language use, things get turned around. We say things because of the external contexts and our strategies to work with them to get what we and the others need. So *language use is an external tool we use* to negotiate social and historical contexts rather than something we possess inside us. We can, therefore, change beliefs and attitudes quickly, but, if we cannot, then that says something very important about our external social contexts and their stability rather than about us and our inner possessions and truths. Once again, if you are having difficulty *thinking this*, then go back and revise the metaphors.

Let me give an example of some of the stories we tell each other: rumors, 'serious knowledge', science stories, medical stories, grotesque medical stories, urban legends, folk legends, and gossip. How and why we tell such stories is usually 'explained' from some properties arising from within us. Most typically, the explanation is given along these lines: We have fear from events, anxiety, and conflicts within us and the function of telling such stories is to remove or 'catharsize' that fear and conflict (Guerin, 2001a, 2001b; Guerin & Miyazaki, 2006). This way of thinking goes back a long way and normally people and academics go along with it (Freud got hooked in by this as well).

If we make our 180° shift from what we normally think, we need to rethink the telling of those stories as *social negotiations with external controls*: we are doing something to people that might bring about friendship and attachment or get us something more specific in some cases, perhaps. If we are not telling them to catharsize our angst, then why tell those stories? Why not spend our conversations telling stories that are not frightful or denigrating to the subjects of gossip and slander? Moreover, why do we keep telling them to new audiences if the earlier telling was supposed to have catharsized any fear or anxiety? Did it not work if we keep on repeating our horror stories?

The point of course is that the properties of such stories – widespread anxiety and fear, social derision, in short – are all properties of making good, interesting stories which are utilized socially rather than springing out of an inner well. For example, the rumors *use* anxiety (rather than catharsize it) to get and keep the listener's attention, but they need to be short unless a story format is used that has properties to prolong a story without losing interest. Rumors then become more like urban and folk legends and conspiracy theories. Unlike gossip, the stories involved in rumors cannot hold attention just because of the persons being discussed, because only a limited number of people will know the person in the rumor, so the subject matter needs to be relevant (consequential, important) to the listener in other ways. Rumors are no good if they are not of consequence to the listener: "I heard a rumor the other day that there are people in the UK who buy houses" – boring! Gossip holds attention because it is made juicy (elements that are exaggerated or fictitious make little difference usually) and can involve people known to almost everyone, like celebrity gossip.

The conclusion from these rethinkings is that there are no separate forms of stories given to us from the world; rather, what we label different forms of stories depend on the conversational (social) properties they use to engage a listener (Guerin & Miyazaki, 2006). This means that you can always adapt a story and add some property (maybe even ones like acting out a part of it) to engage the listener. Whether it belongs to a conventionally labeled category of conversational story or is a hybrid is not important – they are all variations, because of their properties.

The main point from this brief example, then, is that getting a gut feel for the *external*, *virtual*, and *social* properties of language use changes how we view our worlds of talking. It puts the focus out there externally in the details of the contexts in which we talk and live. Many researchers have already explored much of this, notably conversational and discursive analysts (see Guerin, 2004), but much remains to do – especially linking the language use strategies to more of the social and historical contextual details.

The point, then, is that the social strategies of using language in the example are really about the external social context built into other contexts involving history, culture, and relationships. You cannot understand these language use strategies by trying to focus solely on the meaning or syntax of the words and phrases.

One final point. I have focused exclusively in this chapter on language, as a trained and organized way to get things done with other people. There are other related ways people can be trained together so they respond in similar (or at least predictable) ways. There is not room to say more here, but these include what we label 'symbols'. Symbols follow the same ideas sketched above for language; we spend time learning and training people that some thing or event is responded to (perhaps just by thinking) in a particular way (Firth, 1973). Again, there is nothing mysterious about this, even if those using symbols want it to look mysterious.

The examples arise when we have a group who spend time together over a long period (perhaps generations), and especially when in isolation from others, and develop specific ways of responding to things and events that only they are trained to do. We generically call these 'cultural', but that covers many different versions, many different social contexts ('pop culture'?), and many different sorts of groups of people.

References

Anscombe, G. E. M. (1958). On brute facts. *Analysis*, 18, 69–72.

Aronsson, K., & Cekaite, A. (2011). Activity contracts and directives in everyday family politics. *Discourse & Society*, 22, 137–154.

Bentley, A. F. (1935). *Behavior knowledge fact*. Bloomington, IN: Principia Press.

Bentley, A. F. (1941/1975). The human skin: Philosophy's last line of defense. *Philosophy of Science*, 8, 1–19 (reprinted in Bentley, 1954/1975).

Bentley, A. F. (1954/1975). *Inquiry into inquiries: Essays in social theory*. Westport, CT: Greenwood Press.

Carey, T. (2008). *Hold that thought! Two steps to effective counseling and psychotherapy with the method of levels*. St. Louis, MO: Newview.

Chown, M. (2007). *Quantum theory cannot hurt you: A guide to the universe*. London: Faber and Faber.

Cicourel, A. V. (1973). *Cognitive sociology: Language and meaning in social interaction*. London: Penguin Books.

Deleuze, G. (1953). *Empiricism and subjectivity: An essay on Hume's theory of human nature*. New York: Columbia University Press.

Deleuze, G. (2004). *Desert islands and other texts. 1953–1974*. New York: Semiotext(e).

Eder, D., & Enke, J. L. (1991). The structure of gossip: Opportunities and constraints on collective expression among adolescents. *American Sociological Review*, 56, 494–508.

Einstein, A. (1924/2007). *Relativity: The special and general theory*. East Bridgewater, MA: Signature Press.

Firth, R. (1973). *Symbols: Public and private*. Ithaca, NY: Cornell University Press.

Freud, S. (1910/1925). The antithetical sense of primal words. In *The Collected papers of Sigmund Freud* (Vol. IV, pp. 184–191). London: Hogarth Press.

Freud, S. (1915/1984). *The unconscious* (Penguin Freud Library Vol. 11). London: Penguin Books.

Freud, S. (1925/1984). *Negation* (Penguin Freud Library Vol. 11). London: Penguin Books.

Gee, J. P. (1992). *The social mind: Language, ideology, and social practice*. NY: Bergin & Garvey.

Gibson, J. J. (1979). *The ecological approach to visual perception*. Boston: Houghton Mifflin.

Goffman, E. (1974). *Frame analysis*. New York: Harper & Row.

Guerin, B. (1997). How things get done: Socially, non-socially; with words, without words. In L. J. Hayes & P. Ghezzi (Eds.), *Investigations in behavioral epistemology* (pp. 219–235). Reno, NV: Context Press.

Guerin, B. (2001a). Replacing catharsis and uncertainty reduction theories with descriptions of the historical and social context. *Review of General Psychology*, 5, 44–61.

Guerin, B. (2001b). Individuals as social relationships: 18 ways that acting alone can be thought of as social behavior. *Review of General Psychology*, 5, 406–428.

Guerin, B. (2003). Language use as social strategy: A review and an analytic framework for the social sciences. *Review of General Psychology*, 7, 251–298.

Guerin, B. (2004). *Handbook for analyzing the social strategies of everyday life*. Reno, NV: Context Press.

Guerin, B. (forthcoming). *Understanding people through social contextual analysis: A practical guide*. Abingdon: Routledge.

Guerin, B., & Miyazaki, Y. (2006). Analyzing rumors, gossip, and urban legends through their conversational properties. *Psychological Record*, 56, 23–34.

Harré, R. (Ed.) (1976). *Life sentences: Aspects of the social role of language*. New York: John Wiley.

Hayes, S. C., Strosahl, K. D., & Wilson, K. G. (2012). *Acceptance and commitment therapy: The process and practice of mindful change* (2nd ed.). New York: Guilford Press.

Kantor, J. R. (1981). *Interbehavioral philosophy*. Chicago: Principia Press.

Lodhi, S., & Greer, R. D. (1989). The speaker as listener. *Journal of the Experimental Analysis of Behavior*, 51, 353–360.

Matthews, R. (2005). *25 big ideas: The science that's changing our world*. Oxford: Oneworld Publications.

Mills, C. W. (1940). Situated actions and vocabularies of motive. *American Sociological Review*, 5, 904–913.

Modée, J. (2000). Observation sentences and joint attention. *Synthese*, 124, 221–238.

Perls, F. (1969). *Gestalt therapy verbatim*. Lafayette, CA: Real People Press.

Potter, J. (2006). Cognition and conversation. *Discourse Studies*, 8, 131–140.

Quine, W. V. O. (1968). Ontological relativity. *Journal of Philosophy*, 65, 185–212.

Quine, W. V. O. (1974). *The roots of reference*. La Salle, IL: Open Court.

Reps, P. (1957). *Zen flesh, Zen bones*. Harmondsworth, Middlesex: Penguin Books.

Rosaldo, R. (1989). *Culture & truth: The remaking of social analysis*. Boston: Beacon Press.

Ryan, M.-L. (2001). *Narrative as virtual reality: Immersion and interactivity in literature and electronic media*. London: The Johns Hopkins University Press.

Sartwell, C. (2000). *End of story: Toward an annihilation of language and history*. New York: State University of New York Press.

Searle, J. R. (1995). *The construction of social reality*. New York: The Free Press.

Skinner, B. F. (1957). *Verbal behavior*. Englewood Cliffs, NJ: Prentice Hall.

te Molder, H., & Potter, J. (Eds.). (2005). *Conversation and cognition*. Cambridge, UK: Cambridge University Press.

Thomas, W. I., & Thomas, D. S. (1928). *The child in America: Behavior problems and programs*. New York: Knopf.

Wertsch, J. V. (1985). *Vygotsky and the social formation of mind*. London: Harvard University Press.

4 Thinking, self-talk, and how to read minds

In this chapter we will focus on what is usually thought about as the 'inner person'. We have seen how social contexts (albeit a complex version) are the conditions for behavior to emerge, and in the last chapter we saw that talking and language use are also brought about socially, even though they seem intensely private. We will now look at the talking we do with ourselves, the editing that is done, and how our external social contexts control all this 'self-talk'. Part of the exercise will also be to explain these questions: why it is that we seem to do things because of an 'inner' urge or desire; why we seem to have a private life totally divorced from anyone else; and why I would want to convince you that this is all wrong when it seems so obvious!

Others, for example Deleuze in the quotation that follows, also see the need to begin thinking about thinking in new ways:

> Hume, Bergson, and Proust interest me so much because in their work can be found profound elements for a new image of thought. There's something extraordinary in the way they tell us: thinking means something else than what you believe. We live with a particular image of thought, that is to say, before we begin to think, we have a vague idea of what it means to think, its means and ends. And then someone comes along and proposes another idea, a whole other image .... Yes, what we're looking for these days is a new image of the act of thought, its functioning, its genesis in thought itself.
>
> (Deleuze, 2004, pp. 139–140)

My aim, then, is that when you are analyzing the thinking you do, the thoughts you have, the way those thoughts change and adapt, and how those thoughts play a role in your life, you will have the skills and metaphorical help to analyze all that thinking behavior as something controlled through your very complex social and other external contexts.

Not as originating from 'within' you, as it were. And when people tell you their thoughts or you infer they are thinking, you will have the skills to actually 'see' their external contexts or know to ask about them, rather than attribute internal origins and fictitious 'inner' workings to the thoughts (with help from contextual observation and holistic elephants).

To start, though, let me summarize the difficult bits of the last two chapters using J. J. Gibson's ideas of perception as a new example or case study. In studying perception, Gibson was (like the present book, Chapter 1) trying to get away from the position of not being able to say anything about perception before we have fully explained how light gets in the eyes, turns into 'sensations', and then into 'perceptions', etc., down the chain. He tried to change the metaphor into one in which people are directly 'attuned' to what is 'afforded' by the environment because of their histories, and, like in my earlier metaphor, affordances seem to resonate us like waves as we move about the environment and do things to it, rather than hit our eyes like a billiard ball.

So when I approach a chair, instead of having to explain first how I compute all the sensations of that chair into a perception and a cognition, etc., the approach I battled in Chapter 1, Gibson metaphored that we 'directly perceive' not 'the chair', but the affordances of that chair – sitting, lifting, tipping over, etc. (Gibson, 1979; Guerin, 1990). Notice that this correctly focuses our study on the contextual properties of the world and what is afforded by the world, that is, on *describing fully the contexts in which we live, rather than on the micro-physics in which we live* (as particle metaphors would).

Now, what of Chapters 2 and 3? What we have seen, looked at in these terms, is that *Gibson missed out the ubiquitous socialness of all these events*, including chairs (except for some hints he gave: 1979, pp. 42, 135). This is now elucidated by the Chapter 2 material. When I walk up to a chair, the chair affords sitting, etc., as above, but the chair also affords a whole slew of *social actions* that fit into *social strategies* – asking if your friend wants to sit down, looking for a second chair for your friend, stealing the chair because your poor old mother has no chairs in her house, asking someone where they got those really nice chairs from and how much they cost, telling a funny story about when you fell off a chair once, etc. In Gibson's terms, the point of Chapter 2 was to illustrate that social affordances probably outnumber non-social affordances, or even that there might be no totally non-social affordances – which is one of the main useful points to learn from many of the social constructionists' writings.

Now notice the examples of social affordances from the chair, above. In Gibson's terms, what we then learned from Chapter 3 was that *most of all* – and I want to really emphasize *most of all – the environment affords us talking to people.* Explaining things, answering questions, showing off, remembering to tell later, etc. This really puts Chapters 2 and 3 together. Most things and events are social and the major social affordance of 'perception' is talking to others. Both might arise from a chair as context but their pathways are very different.

In this chapter we will now begin putting all these ideas together to get a better contextual idea of what is going on when we *talk about our self* or *our beliefs* or when we *think*. We have common-sense metaphors about these which psychology has adopted uncritically on the whole, but the main metaphor from the 1960s onwards has been that 'cognitive processes' take place within our brains, and that these processes do the thinking and believing events, or they are those events. I do not want to throw out all the research on cognition but, rather, to give it a new metaphor that is in line with a contextual view of how things operate in the world (Guerin, 2001a, 2001b). This does not reject any cognitive data, just reframes them (fairly radically, I must admit ...).

Part of this is going to comprise some of the weirdest of the 180° changes in rethinking in this entire book, so here and elsewhere (Chapter 5) I will give you more places to read others who have said the same or similar things. To give you a heads-up, here are the sorts of things I am going to write:

- All thoughts are intrusive thoughts.
- We are always having multiple thoughts, not just a single stream.
- What we think of as consciousness is just our unspoken language preparation or editing (a resonating talking action).
- The single stream of 'consciousness' seems singular (or single channel) only because it is speech rehearsal and we can only *say* one thing at a time.
- All our thoughts are from the 'unconscious' but the unconscious is just the outside world/context we engage with and have engaged with in the past – not some grey, gooey area inside our heads.
- Beliefs, attitudes, and opinions are social strategies that use language and are not reports on inner states.
- We do not 'repress' thoughts; the world (our contexts) does that.
- 'Cognitive processing' means talking to oneself and emerges from our social contexts, not from within.
- 'Controlled thought processes' mean the ones being edited or rehearsed to say to people whereas automatic cognitive processes are the other multiple and concurrent thoughts or the unconscious.

- Thoughts or consciousness do not control our actions – they are preparation to say things to people, sometimes out loud eventually.
- But despite all the above, thoughts sure do *seem* to control our actions.

In other words, hold on to your hats! This will be radical.

The ideas I will cover have been suggested by many other thinkers, but usually without showing how they fit into a bigger picture of social life strategies (Cooley, 1909; Cushman, 1990; Deleuze, 1991; Dennett, 1969; Erickson, Rossi, & Rossi, 1976; Gee, 1992; Jones, 2009; Josephs & Valsiner, 1998; Kantor, 1981; Kennedy, 1998; Mead, 1934; Nietzsche, 1967; Peirce, 1955; Rapaport, 1955; Rose, 1996, 1998; Sampson, 1993; Sartre, 1937/1991; Stanley, 2012; Suzuki, 1969; Watson, 1924; Wertsch, 1985; Wittgenstein, 1958). I will be drawing on these writings but this book is not about reviewing all these past ideas but utilizing them to give you new thinking skills.

> For most philosophers the ego is an 'inhabitant' of consciousness. Some affirm its formal presence at the heart of *Erlebnisse*, as an empty principle of unification. Others – psychologists for the most part – claim to discover its material presence, as the center of desires and acts, in each moment of our psychic life. We should like to show here that the ego is neither formally nor materially in consciousness: it is outside, in the world. It is a being of the world, like the ego of another.
>
> (Sartre, 1937/1991, p. 31)

In this chapter I will first talk through some important points about thoughts and thinking, exploring what others have drawn from these ideas and the metaphors we have met in this book. From this I will summarize seven key points that you should try and get a gut feeling for, even if the full implications take longer. Then I will explore what these different types of thinking or 'social conversations' are (what they do to other people) and who the audiences might be, taking material from many different thinking traditions. Finally, I will give some examples as guiding points on how to use this material in terms of 'talking' therapies and cognitive behavior therapies and the more recent versions of this. I believe that adding the external social context as the main determinant of (context for) our multiple thoughts will lead to some important breakthroughs in how to treat 'thinking' disorders in therapy – both everyday thinking and pathological. And yes, somewhere in there I will also explain how you can read people's minds. Really, it requires patience but no magic.

Rethinking thoughts and thinking

Thinking and causality

What I am going to be giving you a feel for first is that all our 'inner' or 'private' thinking and ideas and images are not actually 'inside' us at all in any sense – they occur because they are contextualized by events external to our body. You will need to keep remembering and applying the wave and resonance metaphors from Chapter 2. In everyday life, however, we have a strong sense of just the opposite – that our self-talk is somehow inside us and directly controls our behavior. I will show you some opposite ways to think this, however. For example, when we do things we usually have commentary going on, perhaps preparing or rehearsing for someone else's comments afterwards. We might say things 'in our head' as if we are telling people the things we are doing. But this habitually then appears to us as if that talking to ourselves is *causing* us to do the action, whereas it was happening anyway under the control of another context that is present, usually external social contexts.

> The human intuition concerning the priority of thought over behaviour is worth just about as much as our human intuition that the earth is flat.
>
> (Harris, 1979, p. 60)

So for example, a while ago I dropped the soap while in the shower but my hand snapped out and caught it before it hit the ground. At the same time, or just as I grabbed it, actually, I was saying or preparing to talk about this, as if to someone. However, *the strong feeling I had was that I had told myself to grab the soap and that my talking caused my hand to move out and grab it*. Upon reflection, though, it was very, very clear that this would have been too slow and if I had verbally *caused* myself to grab the soap I would have missed it by miles. But the point here is that although it really seemed like the talking preparation to myself was *causing* me to direct my hand to do what it did, this was definitely not the case. It was the *social* resonances that brought about the 'thinking', not the soap – what I would have said if an audience had been there.

It obviously still seems as if our preparatory talking causes our body to behave. Some reasons for why we might believe that our thinking causes our actions were nicely put in introducing Acceptance and Commitment Therapy (ACT). Hayes and Sackett (2005, pp. 1–5) point out that as children we are told that we can control our 'emotions' and 'thoughts': "Stop crying, control yourself!", "Just try and forget about her!" We are also led to believe that we can hide certain behaviors and that this is like putting them inside of us: "Don't tell anyone what you are thinking. Keep it deep inside you." Finally, some of this all seems to work, and we think we can control what we do by 'will-power'. But often this is just through processes of (external) distraction, and the words are in fact being directed from social sources (like all the examples in this paragraph).

So the first guiding point is that we need to assume that so-called 'inner' talk, self-talk, or private talk are actually forms of preparatory social conversations that are resonating from some sort(s) of audiences who are probably not present, just as we saw for the 'outside' talking and conversations with audiences in the last chapter. As Watson put it: "what the psychologists have hitherto called thought is in short nothing but talking to ourselves" (Watson, 1924, p. 238). In order to drastically rethink what we know about thinking, this is the starting point for you to explore.

> Memory, like belief, like all psychological phenomena, is an action; essentially, it *is the action of telling a story.* Almost always we are concerned here with a linguistic operation, quite independent of our attitude towards the happening. A sentinel outside the camp watches the coming of the enemy. When the enemy arrives, the first business of the sentinel is to perform particular actions related to this arrival; he must defend himself or must hide, must lie flat, crawl in order to escape notice, and make his way back to the camp. These are actions of adaptation demanded by the event, and the perception of an event is nothing else than the totality of such acts of adaption. But simultaneously with these acts of adaptation, the sentinel must exhibit a reaction of a new kind, a kind which is characteristic of memory; he must prepare a speech, must in accordance with certain conventions translate the event into words, so that he may be able ere long to tell his story to the commander. This second reaction has important peculiarities which differentiate it markedly from the first reaction. The actions which comprised this, the action of self-defence, that of lying flat, that of hiding in one way or another, are no doubt preserved like all the tendencies; but they can only be reproduced, can only be activated anew, if the sentinel is again placed in the same circumstances, being faced by the same enemy and upon the same ground; they will not be reproduced in different circumstances, as for instance when the sentinel has gone back to camp, is among his comrades, and in the presence of his commander. On the other hand, the second reaction, his account of the matter, though it likewise is after a fashion adapted to the event,

> can readily be reproduced under new conditions when the sentinel is among his comrades in the presence of the commander, and when there is no sign of the enemy. The stimulus which will arouse the activation of this tendency is a special form of social action, a *question*. Thus the essential characteristic of the sentinel's story is that it is independent of the event to which it relates, whereas the reactions which comprise his perception have no such independence.
>
> (Janet, 1919/1925, pp. 661–662)

Thoughts refigured as virtual reality: the external social control over thoughts

To think differently about thinking we need to go back to the last chapter and the identity of language use and virtual reality, where the 'connecting' elements were other people. We cannot do anything to cats by merely talking about them; we can do something to cats, however, by telling other people to do things to cats (which might work in certain contexts).

Metaphor 10. Thinking can also be reimagined as virtual reality

One way to think about thinking in this way is to imagine that the surgeon from Chapter 3 is now operating on his/her own back with the virtual reality surgery machine, also from Chapter 3. We will assume some anesthetics are working. What would happen? Would the surgeon get the illusion that they are directly putting their hands into their back and doing surgical things? And directly *causing* the effects? If so, and more importantly for our purposes, would they also forget that to operate on their own back *they still need to work through the whole second virtual reality machine*? So to them it might not seem that the whole external apparatus is doing the work or is even involved. This is how you might try and think why it is we feel like we think our own thoughts but we have forgotten that they only occur because of other people and social conversations and strategies – we forget there is always the second machine involved.

While we do not know what this self-surgery would really feel like, the situation described is one way of thinking about thinking or self-talk as being controlled externally and socially even though it feels as if we are doing all of it internally or directly, usually attributed to happenings in the head. So if you can imagine that the self-operating surgeon feels like they are directly manipulating or touching or slicing their own back when they move the gloves, even though in fact the operation is taking place via a whole other machine, then this is how I want you to think about your own thoughts. They are being brought about (are resonating) by a confluence of social contexts and relationships external to you, they rely on other people for resonance, but these actions then appear to be acting independently of anyone else and be somehow internal to you. In the same way that words do not control directly the things of events they seem to be referring or corresponding to, so the thinking about oneself or one's own actions (as the referent or correspondent) does not control 'oneself', since the whole talking system is primarily brought about by social relationships externally.

Put bluntly, if we say "That cat is going to stand up" over and over to a cat lying down we will not cause the cat to stand up (assuming we do not just scare it by calling out loudly or something). Likewise, if we say over and over again "I am not going to eat any more chocolates tonight" while sitting in front of three blocks of chocolate we will have limited success in resisting eating more. What success we might have, however, will be from any external social contexts for that language use (the second machine involved), rather than anything like 'an inner self-control'. In terms of the resonance metaphor, our normal feelings about our thoughts are like that of being a guitar having its strings resonate from another nearby, exactly tuned guitar, but we (the guitar) then think that we created these resonating notes by ourselves from within our guitarhood consciousness.

This last sentence and the virtual reality idea both give us a clue for people exercising self-control: you must make the words you say to yourself *work properly through the other virtual reality machine* (in this case, other people) and not assume that just moving the gloves is going to do anything at all to operate on your back if the second machine is switched off.

Thoughts as associations: replacing this oldest metaphor

One of the oldest metaphors for thinking and cognition is that bits of the outside world, or sensations, perceptions, ideas, impressions, etc., form associations, networks, or some form of linking with 'thoughts' inside the head and this is the material that is then processed (cognitive), stamped in (Thorndike), reinforced (Hull), etc. So the many relationships out there in the world become mapped or represented as networks inside the head or brain. Intuitively this makes sense, and I am not going to say that people for thousands of years have been stupid. They have not been. For instance, when I say "Cat" most people say "Dog," which certainly suggests people have internal associations formed between these two ideas, or stimuli, or aural sensations, or something.

Note, however, that this is a *particle metaphor*, and so people are then led to metaphoring that the ideas, impressions or cognitions can interfere with each other like billiard balls or particles. Inside our head then becomes a metaphorical battleground of conflicting thoughts that reside there somewhere. Of course, having read Chapter 3 and encountered the virtual reality idea it is clear that any 'word associations' are actually formed through other people (in training the second machine) and are the result of external social training. The 'cat' and the 'dog' are linked out there in the social world and our history of that world of trained English-language users (in my case), not inside our heads. The association, if we still wish to call it that, is out there in the world and the history in the world, not inside your head as particles stored safely away until recalled (Deleuze, 1991).

This much should be clear from both Chapters 2 and 3 and the metaphors described there. However, I want to say some more about the 'particle' aspect of the 'association' and the 'cognitive processing' part of all this. And that will be done by reusing or economically recycling the 'waves versus particle' metaphor from Chapter 2 and applying it now to thinking itself.

Metaphor 11. Thoughts are like the effects of waves rather than emitted particles

When we last left our receiving/transmission tower in Chapter 2 it had all these mobile phone waves going through it and the tower would respond if correctly 'attuned' – respond immediately and not after thinking about it. In our case, the attunement involves our relationships and actions with resources or interests, and a history of those waves and the consequences of responding. However, one of the most common things that happens with people when there are contexts around them exerting wave-like influence (figuratively), is that there is language use. We saw in Chapter 2 that most of our contextual waves are social – they involve people. We then saw in Chapter 3 that when people exert a wave-like influence as contextual waves, one extremely common thing we have all learned to do is to say something, to talk about it.

The metaphor now could go something like this. Many or most waves that pass through the tower attune at least one action: but at the minimum they are attuned to generate some words as responding – whether or not the main responding of passing on the telephone call goes ahead. Our most important resonance to any waves (any social influence) is to prepare multiple spoken responses.

So, we now have the vision of wave-like influences around us most of the time, almost all of which are social context waves, and we have many of these being attuned into a form to use as language, although most of these do not occur out loud. The main reason for all this is historical – social context is ubiquitous and mediates most of our resources and interests, and much of the wave traffic with other people involves using language rather than directly affecting them or interacting with them. So our most frequent actions are to talk or think.

Now here is where it gets interesting … If there are other appropriate context waves present then there is a murky morass of thought reactions which have not been 'thought' yet, but which are sitting there like a background pile of dark matter (this will be called the 'unconscious'). With multiple resonances, these thoughts can get changed in different ways, and the rest of this chapter is about some of the ways we believe they get changed. They can happily sit together and not conflict (as particles would), but they might be resonating opposing talk or other actions.

We must not, at this point, revert to pre-Chapter 1 status and think that the tower 'processes' and decides to rehearse some of these thought reactions that have not been 'thought'. Whatever occurs in or out of the tower happens because there are external contexts that make those things happen. Just like any action or thought, whether or not it happens is brought about by the external contexts exerting influence, not because of a whimsical decision made internally by a tower.

The final point to make is that in everyday life the vast majority of 'thought reactions' do not get 'thought', inasmuch as they are usually not noticed under normal conditions, which is why Freud and others before and after him have used the term 'unconscious'. I have problems with this word because it gives the metaphorical impression of being a particle thing, being in a place, being controlled by the body, and being unitary – in all, the unconscious as talked about by academics seems to be a place for particles to congregate or huddle while waiting to gain thoughthood or to be rehearsed and become 'conscious' on a stage, somehow. I also have problems with the word 'conscious', for very similar reasons to those given for 'unconscious', plus one new problem – that calling a thought 'conscious' or talking about having a thought 'in consciousness' also gives two strong metaphorical impressions that I believe are wrong: (1) there is a 'you' in control of these thoughts and possessing them, and (2) that they go on to control the behavior they seem to be referring to. In Chapter 3 we tried to put aside ideas that language use directly (without other people; without the second virtual reality machine) controlled what they seemed to be talking about, and here we are doing the same change in thinking for the retalking 'thoughts'.

So I will now spell out these points in more detail, without the metaphors most of the time. But from this metaphor I hope you can start making the 180° shift to thinking that:

- There are social relationship (and other) contexts (waves) which affect us (resonate), not stimuli (particles).
- We need to think of these as affecting us if we are attuned to them with wave-like properties rather than as causal particles.
- Most contexts that affect us involve social contexts with a history and this happens even when alone (Chapter 2), although having someone in front of you focuses them more.
- Actions (including doing something, talking, or preparing to talk – 'thinking') are resonated-by-attunement to these contexts because of a history of past attunements and the interests or resources as outcomes they had, usually via the social contexts: the environment for this is not static (not moment-by-moment real-time processing).
- Whatever the past attunements, many of the context waves also generate-by-attunement other actions that we would do/speak if we were to use language to someone (whether we do or not mostly depends on other contexts being present).
- One (or some?) of these sometimes gets rehearsed (as it were) as if we were speaking it or about to speak it.
- These 'thoughts', whether edited, rehearsed, or whatever, do not control other actions which are independently generated-by-attunement – *instead they are generated in potential readiness to speak to people, not as controllers of the actions they seem to describe*.
- These thoughts, however, sure do seem to us as if they are controlling our actions, especially when the same 'waves' are likely to be attuned to both the actions and the talking about the actions.

Seven key points for rethinking thinking

This is all very difficult, and probably new to your thinking skills. So after our first start at rethinking thoughts and thinking, I wish to draw out seven key points from the above to summarize and hopefully consolidate to help you a little.

'We' do not control thinking: all thoughts are intrusive thoughts

> With regard to the superstitions of logicians, I shall never tire of emphasizing a small terse fact, which these superstitious minds hate to concede – namely, that a thought comes when 'it' wishes, and not when 'I' wish, so that it is a falsification of the facts of the case to say that the subject 'I' is the condition of the predicate 'think'. It thinks; but that this 'it' is precisely the famous old 'ego' is, to put it mildly, only a supposition, an assertion, and assuredly not an 'immediate certainty'. After all, one has even gone too far with this 'it thinks' – even the 'it' contains an interpretation of the process, and does not belong to the process itself. One infers here according to the grammatical habit: 'Thinking is an activity; every activity requires an agent; consequently –'
>
> (Nietzsche, 1886/1966, p. 24)

In the same way that words do not control language use, social contexts do, so it is that there is no 'I' that controls thinking. It certainly feels as if there is an 'I' which controls things, and which 'says' things in our head that we can later say out loud, but this is misleading (arising partly from the way we attribute causes: Chapter 1). While this view has been stated many times over the centuries, as the quotation from Nietzsche above does, we still need to specify more about what exactly this 'it' is. In this chapter I have shown that the social context is not just a part of thinking or the cause of thinking, but the very thinking itself – the 'it' itself! *The 'unconscious' is the external world of social and other contexts.*

There are many, many implications of this, however, and we can go even further than this in rethinking our thoughts about thoughts. For example, all thoughts will appear as 'intrusive thoughts', since they all come under external control. For those thoughts that we normally label as 'intrusive thoughts' we must undertake a special analysis to see what makes them stand out from all other thoughts (which I am also now calling intrusive). Some ideas are given in Table 4.1, using an analysis of Freud as the basis.

Table 4.1 Analyzing intrusive thoughts

Following the thinking of Nietzsche outlined earlier, I have suggested above that we should think of *all thoughts as intrusive thoughts*. What, then, is the special contextual analysis of what are normally called 'intrusive thoughts'; what is different about those treated as intrusive? Let us look at an example from Freud (1909/1979, p. 68), who calls them 'compulsive ideas':

In this instance the connection between the compulsive idea and the patient's life is contained in the opening words of his story. His lady was absent [to nurse her grandmother who was seriously ill], *while he was working very hard for an explanation so as to bring the possibility of an alliance with her nearer. While he was working he was overcome by a longing for his absent lady, and he thought of the cause of her absence. And now there came over him something which, if he had been a normal man, would probably have been some kind of feeling of annoyance against her grandmother: "Why must the old woman get ill just at the very moment when I'm longing for her so frightfully?" We must suppose that something similar but far more intense passed through our patient's mind – an unconscious fit of rage which could combine with his longing and find expression in the exclamation: "Oh, I should like to go and kill that old woman for robbing me of my love!" Thereupon followed the command: "Kill yourself, as a punishment for these savage and murderous passions!" The whole process then passed into the obsessional patient's consciousness accompanied by the most violent affect and* in a reverse order – *the punitive command coming first, and the mention of the guilty outburst afterwards.*

The patient went on to become confused by his concurrent and non-conflicting compulsive thoughts between suicide and murdering the grandmother, but he mainly reproached himself for even thinking to kill the grandmother. In the normal view of things (particle thinking) we might conclude that he must have really 'wanted' to kill the grandmother because he thought it. If we think, instead, that there was a strong desire (for whatever reasons) for his lady and also a strong desire that she not go and attend her grandmother, then in terms of multiple thoughts we can imagine that there might have been all sorts of strategies playing around (resonating) in his behavior and his thinking for ways out of this conflict.

What is perhaps the real pathology and hence 'intrusiveness' in all this is: that he took these fleeting thoughts so seriously; did not have a defense or strategies against them; that his obsession with his lady was probably overwrought; that other bits of his case history suggests that if his 'alliance' with this lady fell through his life was going to be in very bad shape; that his thinking might have been utilizing a dramatic or histrionic strategy, hoping someone would intervene and stop him by making things magically right again. The point here is that there is so much more in the external social context going on that helps us understand and single out what is happening to this man's thinking, and why he was not merely annoyed at the situation like most of us would be.

If I had been Freud, I would have questioned this man in much the same way but would have put more emphasis on who he thought might have been *the audiences* for both these thoughts: "*Oh, I should like to go and kill that old woman for robbing me of my love!*" and "*Kill yourself, as a punishment for these savage and murderous passions!*" Who did he imagine he might have said these to and with what imagined effects from those people? Why take them so seriously?

Also, once we see the external social context as providing the contexts for our thoughts (as if talking to oneself), there is no reason why there must only be a single strand to all this. We are always *resonating with multiple thoughts*, not just a single stream (I like to call these 'thinklings'). Many events are being contextualized, especially if two conflicting audiences are either present or being contextualized. This is no different than for all our other behaviors being influenced (resonated) by multiple contexts simultaneously and somewhat independently (remember that waves do not interfere). In Chapter 2, I tried an analogy based on electromagnetic waves to help you rethink these behaviors. For now, we can have multiple influences producing multiple 'thoughts' even though only one usually is 'conscious' or being 'talked' or rehearsed.

My point is that our *talking to ourselves* or conversing to ourselves about one wave of these thoughts might be limited to a single stream, but the contextualizing of thoughts can be happening in multiples all along, leading to mysterious (and sometimes genius-looking) thinking performances. As an example from an early work on thoughts processes:

> The analysis of the content of a train of thought is not completed by the description of the thoughts contained in it .... Besides thoughts, yet other knowledge is present in our thinking. For instance, we know whether or not we are on the right track; whether or not we are approaching our goal; whether or not the thought occurs to us for the first time or derives from memory; we may know even where we have picked it up; we know how it is related to the one preceding. This knowledge only rarely becomes an independent psychic act; we do not specifically focus on its content. It lies, so to say, in between thoughts.
>
> (Buehler, 1951, p. 40)

This means that there can be a constant resonance of many thoughts and 'inapparent' (Hayes, 1994) activities but only some of which 'we' talk about to ourselves or say to ourselves (as it were). They are going on all the time but only some are 'said' to ourselves or rehearsed as if we were talking to others. This is like a kind of background 'dark matter' almost, or, as I suggested in Chapter 2, like background electromagnetic waves. This is the *unconscious* used as metaphor by Freud and many before him (Borch-Jacobsen & Shamdasani, 2012), and these are my *thinklings*. We are always having multiple resonances but only some (because of context) get edited or rehearsed (see below for more on these), and only some (because of the context) get spoken out loud.

It is all too easy here to drag in another decision-making or information-processing center: there is an 'Editor' who deals with the multitude of thoughts constantly appearing and reappearing (resonating) and decides on the basis of some algorithm which one of these eventually gets thought 'consciously' and which others get repressed and which others gets enacted. Freud got close to saying this, in fact, and we had to resist this avenue when dealing with your mobile phone receiving/transmission tower in Chapter 1. But all this is taking place outside in the social and other contexts, not inside. The outside context, mainly social relationship strategies, brings about all these things, and provides our analyses. That is where the conflicting social pressures come from. We do not have stored conflicting thoughts; we have external conflicting audiences and other resonances. 'We' do not even repress thoughts, the external relations do that: 'it' does, as Nietzsche might have said.

Words are not controlled by what is named and neither are thoughts

We saw in Chapter 3 that what controls saying or reading the word 'cat' is not a cat. Words are controlled by the social and other contexts, not by what might be being talked about at the time. If we often say 'cat' when a cat walks in the room this is still from social contexts: why say anything at all otherwise; why 'state the obvious'? How many times has a cat walked in the room and you have not said or thought 'cat'? What in the external social context is different, therefore, when you do? (I find musing over this really helps me to see thinking as external.)

We now come to applying this to thoughts. A thought to do with cats is not controlled by cats. The resonances come not from a cat but from a person or another social context. If there is something to respond to with a cat, such as patting, feeding, being scared, etc., then we just respond. If we have to talk or think about it, then these extra activities have to do with social contexts, not the cat (since the cat will not understand or be affected by our talking or our thinking). Read this well; it is the source of Western philosophical errors for centuries and will be spelled out more in Chapter 5 and the Appendix.

This is a problem in a few realms of life. One is in therapy, when a person has a thought such as, 'I am useless', and they also have a concurrent thought that having the first thought must be controlled by their own uselessness – it is therefore irrefutable. This is equivalent, do you see, to thinking that the cat controls your thinking about the cat. Some of the Third Wave therapies even work directly on changing this. Acceptance and Commitment Theory (ACT), for example, *defuses* 'cognition' from what is named into observing and describing the contexts for those thoughts – changing 'I am useless' to 'I am thinking I am useless', which can then be explored more productively in its context.

In terms of life, we act even though we are most frequently not sure where these acts are coming from – we generally do not know what confluence of contexts is resonating at any time to set thinklings popping into our head. We muddle on and do things, and if we have to explain (to someone), we have a whole realm of metaphors to draw upon that satisfy our listeners.

The same is true of thinking and our thoughts. They are engendered externally to us by context even if we take part in them. But we do not own our thoughts until they happen and we take the consequences; they come to us from all external angles. If I see a cat and think (resonate) of a scene in a book I just read about a cat being killed that does not mean I want to kill a cat or that I like the idea (the thought has me, it is not that I have the thought). I do not have to own that thought and treat it as something about me. It is certainly something about my situation or context (I perhaps should not read books in which a cat gets killed), but as the old cliché says: "Don't believe everything you think"!

Why 'consciousness' is directed towards other people

This is the arena in which we sometimes refer to 'consciousness' and the like, in which one can 'detect' (whatever that means in this sense) multiple thoughts going on but from which only one affordance or resonance gets rehearsed or 'into consciousness', that is, into talking. Which of the multiple thoughts get rehearsed, edited, or said to ourselves as if to others, that is, which are said to be 'conscious', depends solely on the external social contexts from which they resonated in the first place, and this will be a function of the audiences contextualizing those thoughts, the social conflicts, the resources they lead to, past punishments for saying such things out loud, etc. The external audiences for those thoughts determine which 'wins', but in a wave fashion rather than a particle fashion of high-speed billiard balls colliding and causing angst.

How all these resonances of the thinking are combined will be outlined below in more detail. Suffice it to say here that there are multiple events (thinklings) being 'thought' at any one time and some are dealt with in a conversational way and we treat them as causes for our behavior (wrongly) and as 'consciousness'. It becomes obvious that calling all these multiple influences 'thoughts' is misleading, since that term is often reserved for the single 'conscious' one that is being rehearsed or edited as if we are speaking it out loud. This is also why it is good to think of them as resonating waves that are multiple, concurrent, and not in conflict amongst themselves, and why I like to use the word *thinklings* for these background multiple resonating effects that Freud called unconscious thoughts.

> It may seem unbelievable that 'flight of ideas' is more the rule than the exception with us all. Psychoanalytic observation shows that there are two kinds of thought: one is first thought out and then put into words; the other escapes observation before being verbalized .... I picture thinking as a stream of which only the surface is visible; orchestral music of which only the melody is audible.
>
> (Stekel, 1951, pp. 312, 314)

We can also suggest that in dreaming and other noticeable perturbations (see below), this 'dark matter background' of multiple 'thoughts' or resonances that are not rehearsed (are unconscious) has an effect, but without editing. So 'real motives' and wishes are said to be 'expressed' in dreams (Freud, 1900/1975, 1915/1984). This is fine, except that the motives and wishes are not 'inside us' but in those external contextual arrangements of our lives which bring the thoughts into an existence. They are related to the resources and arrangements of people and resources, not to an inner wishing.

Another unusual property to come from all this rethinking of thought is that 'we' do not own, possess, create, or invent our thoughts. This is useful in therapeutic settings, in fact. Imagine that the following thought is 'said' in my 'head' or 'pops into my head' when I see my boss: "I wish he would just go away and die somewhere quietly." People can get upset if they believe 'themselves' to be the inventor, author, or creator of such thoughts and therefore believe that they must *really* wish or *secretly* (to themselves even, unconsciously) want the person to die. They might not even 'think' this as a rehearsal, though, if they edit and repress this thought, according to Freud and others (see below). However, in the view advanced here this is only one train of thinking amongst many that probably resonated upon seeing the boss and that its coming 'to the fore' at all is a property of the audiences present or imagined who have shaped the thought, not of a true, inner self who must wish for this person's death. It might be a joke to colleagues.

As we will find out, in therapeutic practice it is most important to find out who might be the audiences or history resonating such a remark; it could be a joke some work friends have been having together which is not serious, or it could be a game to look tough to other work colleagues and bluff them that you are upwardly mobile, distant, ruthless, or cold. Like the earlier comments on repression, we also need to find out the social contexts in which this one thought out of the many was taken so seriously and over-generalized (e.g. see Beck below).

This fits in nicely with some recent CBT methods of distancing people from their thoughts, especially so-called 'intrusive thoughts', and not making clients take responsibility for every single thought. They might end up taking responsibility for acting and not editing it first, but not for having the thought in the first place. In this sense, then, as Nietzsche hinted in the earlier quotations, *all thoughts are intrusive thoughts* – they all come from outside of us and we do not have an 'ego' that creates, processes, decides, or owns them.

The key questions we need to focus on, following all the above, are:

- Who are the audiences for our different thoughts, since language and hence rehearsal for speaking is socially controlled?
- What part in our social strategies do those thoughts play, including the ones not rehearsed or spoken to yourself but which are still resonating?
- Why do some of the multiple thoughts become the ones rehearsed? What is in the context for that to occur? What is special?

There is another issue that arises with this way of thinking. Sometimes when we are in a conversation a thought comes to us, which we say out loud and then regret. For example, we might be talking about someone's parents and their issues and we say a thought that 'just pops into our heads', such as "Ah just put them into an old folk's home." Now this might have been contextualized (resonated) as a joke with our joking friends as a context, or it might have been related to a conversation you have been having about your parents. But whatever contextualized it, the listener will usually assume that this is what you truly believe, so saying it out loud puts it into the world of serious social consequences. We can see how keeping secrets and 'repression' begin to emerge for thinklings, as avoidance of real consequences for the multiple thoughts that are resonating in our lives.

Thinking is social – it depends on audiences

One of the points to come out in the above is that thinking resonates from social contexts – *but how can we think that; how can we get a good gut feeling for that*? As a starting point we can assume that self-talk is a form of social conversation with some sort(s) of audience, and therefore we can follow the leads from Chapter 3 about talking out loud with people:

- When someone talks, always look for the audiences; what does this talk do to the audiences?

This becomes:

- When someone is thinking or talking to themselves, always look for or ask about the (eventual or historical) audiences for this thinking; who is contextualizing this; who has been resonating these actions?

Let us look more closely now at the idea that external social contexts – people, populations, and audiences – resonate or contextualize our thoughts. After that we will look more closely at the types of things that are done with thoughts (by the world, not by an inner self).

To get the idea of thinking as socially controlled we must work from the ideas in the last chapter about language use and then apply those to talking to ourselves, and then to talking to ourselves about ourselves – the talk of self, ego, and 'I'. The arguments and evidence are that talking to ourselves grows out of talking to others, and keeps many of its properties. But there are some interesting twists to all this.

Of most importance, though, out of these language properties, is that the social control can be general or specific. We might have a whole series of thoughts, or a whole series of stories that are contextualized, or emerge, from the contexts of a specific person. Have you ever met up with an old friend and suddenly you start thinking (resonating) thoughts and words you have not had since you saw them last time?

We might also have the same but for a more abstract, general audience – what sociologists have called for many years the 'generalized other'. That is, we rehearse talk and think talk for a generalized audience, probably typical of those who normally come up against or challenge our talk. Sociologists Cooley (1909) and Mead (1934), in particular, first saw thought as a sort of internalized conversation but which is sometimes directed to a generalized other rather than a specific person we know with an individualized history.

> Self and society are twin-born, we know one as immediately as we know the other, and the motion of a separate and independent ego is an illusion [he goes on to criticize Descartes' *cogito*, as Nietzsche did above].
>
> (Cooley, 1909, p. 5)

> The very process of thinking is, of course, simply an inner conversation that goes on, but it is a conversation of gestures which in

> its completion implies the expression of that which one thinks to an audience. One separates the significance of what he is saying to others from the actual speech and gets it ready before saying it. He thinks it out, and perhaps writes it in the form of a book; but it is still a part of social intercourse in which one is addressing other persons and at the same time addressing one's self, and in which one controls the address to other persons by the response made to one's own gesture.
>
> (Mead, 1934, pp. 141–142)

> The self, as that which can be an object to itself, is essentially a social structure, and it arises as a social experience. After a self has arisen, it in a certain sense provides for itself its social experiences, and so we can conceive of an absolutely solitary self. But it is impossible to conceive of a self arising outside of social experience.
>
> (Mead, 1934, p. 140)

We can now go back to the question posed in the previous section, about having multiple thoughts occurring at any time but only one stream that is 'as if' rehearsed or said but without vocalizing. Putting this together with the role of specific and general audiences, we can suggest that *it is the audiences contextualizing the thoughts that 'compete', not the thoughts.* What exactly determines this is not clear and it could be different aspects at different times. Is it the acceptability of any thoughts to the different audiences; the amount of editing that is needed; the likely consequences with an audience? We will look at various versions of this in the second half of this chapter

To give an example in more detail, consider what someone's 'belief' about euthanasia might be. The mainstream view of psychology and common sense is that they might have considered (processed) information about the issue and made a decision about 'their' belief (usually just for or against). From what was said in the last chapter we can see how this might not correspond with reality. A person 'states' their beliefs for a variety of social functions, but this is not a passive recall or a 'screen dump' of some inner repository of belief and attitude particles. It is a way of saying something to influence listeners (to help establish facts with a listener, which can be a useful strategy for many reasons).

We can now add some more to this analysis. A person will have many 'thoughts' resonating about euthanasia when it is mentioned, including some that are for, some that are against, and others that are about euthanasia but not actually for or against (following the quotation from

Buehler, 1951, given earlier). Included in all these multiple thinklings will be others about the audiences, their past reactions, etc. It could be, however, that only those shaped by our powerful audiences are rehearsed in the talking sense. We might have 'intimations' to ourselves that our 'thinking' is more complex or diverse, but we only rehearse to say to our actual audience the polarized 'for or against' beliefs that are acceptable in social life. This sometimes is glimpsed when we sense we have many thoughts, but either no thoughts are said that are relevant (we are 'tongue tied' sometimes) or else we notice that only one-sided thoughts are said to ourselves and thence out loud if the audience contextualizes this. In this way, 'nothing springs to mind' means that nothing is rehearsed and edited to be able to emerge, rather than meaning that we have no thoughts at all.

This is fairly complex conceptual shifting for the reader, and some more examples and self-observations are almost certainly needed and are given below in the final section. However, I believe this broad way of analyzing 'thinking' is a far better reflection of what actually goes on in our lives than the standard story that 'we' process information, decide upon a belief based upon that information, and then store a list of our beliefs to be retrieved when the topic arises.

(One final interesting line of thought or 'becoming' [Deleuze] for the reader. Going back to an earlier section of Chapter 2 ['How do social relationships pervade our actions, thinking, and self-thinking?'], I think it is no accident that it was sociologists who first pointed out this 'generalized other' audience that contextualizes our thinklings. The shift over the past few centuries from living in close, kin-based communities to our current modernity in which our most frequent and often important relationships are with strangers is, I believe, the origin of the *generalized other*. In kin-based communities the main audiences would have been strictly within families or else an audience of a generalized deity or spirit if it was a religion that was holding the community together as an organizer [Guerin, 1998]. The shift to ubiquitous stranger relationships in modernity has also meant a shift to the common new audience of a generalized other, or better, a generalized stranger relationship, as the one that is resonant, rehearsed, and edited.)

What are the events that happen when we 'think'? The social dynamics of thinking

When we 'think' there are all sorts of events happening, many of which have not been mapped out well because of the emphasis on both the inner sanctity of, and the non-social origins of, thinking. Remember also that 'thinking' often means that we are rehearsing as if we were talking. But even when we are not thinking in this sense ("Sorry, I wasn't really thinking"), there is still a background of thoughts happening (the resonating of thinklings), just as I can notice things going on that I was not concentrating on (not 'rehearsing to say'). In this sense we are always 'thinking', in that we are always resonating to say things even if we are not naming, using, or rehearsing to say what those things are that we are seeing.

Here I want to bring some of this together. The key point is:

> When you are thinking and 'have' thoughts in all their variations, the thoughts have contextual audiences and are social processes with resource outcomes – and they can be done just as well in the absence of those audiences.

For example, on the morning of the day I am writing this I was driving by myself to work when I realized I was thinking about someone I like a lot and ruminating over all sorts of odds and ends to do with that person (there were lots of resonances, bells ringing in my head). That person did not need to actually be there for this, but the influence was still exerted (resonating). We could worry about what minute details 'triggered' (probably this is not even an accurate word here) thinking about that person, but we can get on without doing this (my gravity metaphor). Freud went a little way along these lines and we will learn some of his lessons below. Early behaviorists tried to force a link from sensations to thinking (the usual psychology of a causal sequence from *light to sensation to perception to cognition to motor response to effector response to output*), but this was fruitless, regardless of whether there truly were such links. To my mind, this is like saying that we cannot cut and plane a piece of wood in carpentry until we know all the molecules present in that piece of wood, and in the last chapter we had the gravitation metaphor to rethink this. Chapter 1 dealt with the 'serial decision-making' metaphor that has been used much in psychological thinking.

Some of this was recognized by the Gestalt therapist Fritz Perls (1969), who, when he noticed that the client was having 'inner' conversations, would ask them who they were talking to, or who was doing the talking in their head, and would even get them to 'put' that person in a chair and talk out loud to them as if they were present. This targets in a very practical way one of the most useful analytic approaches, that of analyzing who the audiences are for any thoughts. We need to begin seeing the benefits of contextualizing thoughts properly in order to help understand and change them, and knowing the social and relationships contexts of thoughts is a major step towards this. This is partly what Freud instigated – taking individual strands or resonances of thoughts, even the non-rehearsal ones from dreams (that is, our background resonances, thinklings, or 'unconscious thoughts'), and trying to contextualize them in terms of our audiences. Unfortunately, he was still wedded to the ideas that thinking takes place inside us and not out there, and that the family was the main audience for his clients.

In general, then, the thoughts we have (that resonate), whether ones rehearsed for talking or background ones (conscious or unconscious), depend upon the audiences and the resources engendered through those audiences, and our past history of what those audiences consequated.

> If one suddenly stops and takes note of his thoughts at some time when his mind has been running free, as when he is busy with some simple mechanical work, he will be likely to find them taking the form of vague conversations. This is particularly true when one is somewhat excited with reference to a social situation. If he feels under accusation or suspicion in any way he will probably find himself making a defence, or perhaps a confession, to an imaginary hearer .... Impulsive people often talk out loud when excited, either to 'themselves', as we say when we can see no one else present, or to any one whom they can get to listen. Dreams also consist very largely of imaginary conversations; and, with some people at least, the mind runs in dialogue during the half-waking state before going to sleep.
>
> (Cooley, 1902, p. 90)

> Inner speech is such a ubiquitous aspect of our mental life that, unless it is drawn to our attention, we rarely reflect on it. If you close your eyes and allow your mind to wander, you will discover an almost ceaseless inner chatter swirling within you. Using this inner voice, we comment to ourselves about what is happening to us, silently express our pleasure and dismay, plan what to do next, and censure ourselves whenever we make mistakes.
>
> (Bentall, 2009, p. 178)

Even this quotation, however, is still about doing this to yourself for yourself, rather than in a context of eventual or past audiences. You are even more likely to 'hear' these background thoughts if there is a lack of other sounds.

Just as for any behaviors or activities, the contextual elements such as history, audiences, and outcomes do not have to be present at the exact moment, and we saw that this is prevalent in language use and now we see it for talking-to-oneself. So we end up with the general position that most thinking is rehearsal of stories, excuses, attributions, or actions for real social interaction afterwards, even when alone, and that the listeners or audiences shape these stories, attributions, or actions, but with a resonance metaphor rather than colliding particles in the 'mind'. There are still many forms this can take, as we will see in the second half of this chapter, and how we might actually analyze these contexts in practice will be dealt with elsewhere in more detail (Guerin, forthcoming).

We can read people's thoughts – in a way

In a very limited sense, and not in the sense of popular books and films, we can also read other people's thoughts. Following the terminology given in Chapter 1 of *contextual observation*, so we can anticipate (read) *contextual thoughts*. Once again, this is not doing a direct read from the person's head or psyche, since that is not where thinking is occurring. No Vulcan mind melds here. But if, as argued above, thinking is done out there in the external relationships and other contexts, and not inside the head, then we should be able to anticipate people's thoughts accurately. *We can read people's thoughts but only to the extent that we know their social and historical contexts accurately*. And there is the catch!

This applies to thinking activities as much as any other activities. As mentioned, and as we saw for contextual observation, the accuracy will only be as good as your knowledge of the person's contexts. This is why some people seem to read minds; not because they can do a mind-link or anything science-fictionish, but because they have knowledge and experience in typical people contexts or because they can restrict the current contexts to situations in which they do know what is going on (more like hypnosis).

For example, suppose you had a male client who was an only child in his early teens, and he had lost both parents suddenly in an accident. He was coming to talk to you for the first time since the accident. How can we read his mind, or guess a number of possible thoughts that will all be resonating together for him? While we cannot read these thoughts exactly, in general we can make a number of good guesses and perhaps even appear to be reading his mind. Generically, he will be wondering about you and what you will do, about the loss of his parents, of his future, of getting a girlfriend (or boyfriend if gay), worrying about what other family and school friends will be thinking and assuming about him, etc. None of these have to be true at any one instance, but they are all likely to have been resonating at some point recently. He might also be thinking about the inheritance and might also feel guilty that he is even thinking that occasionally.

All the above is generic context for what has happened and what happens to 'typical' teenage boys. If we were to know something more about his very specific contexts, we could get even closer to 'reading' his thoughts, not in the sense of knowing the actual thoughts he has been having, but in the sense of brainstorming a pool of possible thoughts he might be having, even though they could all be wrong, of course. For example, if he has a steady girlfriend (or boyfriend) then he is likely to be thinking about the effect of his tragedy on the relationship, whether he is to be taken away somewhere far from them, whether they will like him more from sympathy, and again some likely guilt that he has even thought this last thought.

So this is not mind-reading in a popular sense, and it depends on your own life experiences and the amount of context you know for the people involved – and how good you are at brainstorming possibilities (Guerin, forthcoming). None of it is certain but you can usually get fairly close if you think carefully that they will have multiple resonances, both good and bad, and that these resonances will be tied to the main audiences and resources in this person's life. A good counselor or mind-reader might therefore start a conversation: "I suppose you might be worried about what I am going to ask you and whether that will get you taken away to foster care somewhere else?" You are not implying that they definitely have these thoughts, nor that they are responsible for these thoughts if they do, nor that they cannot also have the opposite thoughts concurrently. This is how a good mind-reader works.

Talking about 'inner' processes for utilization as rhetoric

The final point to draw out is about the rhetorical usefulness of the models of 'inner' worlds of thinking and self and action-sources. As we saw in Chapter 3, from a discursive analysis point of view, the everyday uses of talking in these 'mentalistic' ways have some interesting properties. Most importantly, talking about or explaining events in terms of inner causes and the like is a great way to avoid being challenged by listeners. People hearing this talk cannot easily challenge what is said, since it is supposedly 'locked up' inside a person. If I say that I like cats better than dogs it is difficult to make the case that I am mistaken. Referring to 'inner' causes in everyday rhetoric is actually a highly defensible or safe way to talk.

It seems that academics using these same forms of talk also use these same properties to protect their ways of thinking and their models.

Evidence and proof must be indirect, so negative results can also be easily absorbed into a theory. More will be said on this below.

What do we know about contextual strategies of thinking?

Having discussed more about the rethinking of thoughts and thinking, at least in principle, it is now time to explore the more detailed events going on, at least ones that people have proposed at some point. There is a lot we can draw out of people's research and experience, and I want to capture some of that to help your (and my) rethinking of this difficult area. We have a long way to go, and we do not have final answers, just 'becomings'.

Most of these authors I am drawing on here have a standard Western way of thinking about thoughts, either associationist (cognitive or old S-R behavioral) or the more recent versions of cognitive processing. Those based on radical behaviorism are closer. That is okay and I will try to update these, since their ideas and some of their data are still important and valid, even if I cruelly and brutally dismantled their metaphors in my earlier chapters.

Types of audiences and how they affect thinking

Strictly speaking, it is not an audience that contextualizes any thoughts, but the resources accessed through those people, or the joint outcomes possible through networking with those people. But given that many of those resources we have as consequences of our acting and thinking are generalized (the same) across a number of audiences, then this full specification is impossible to analyze in practice in any case.

If we are engaged in talking to someone in front of us then this will clearly affect our thinking in a very immediate way. It would seem especially that any verbally rehearsed thoughts (conscious) are highly likely to be relevant to the current demands, unless it is someone boring or repetitive whom you can listen to and track enough for conversation while also 'thinking' about other things altogether. This is sometimes forgotten, I have noticed, in reports by both therapists and experimental researchers. For example, a therapist might write that they asked the client to think of a positive self-statement and then urged them to say it to themselves once every morning after breakfast. They proceed to write, following this, about how that *thought itself* controlled the early morning conversation with oneself, and the role of the therapist-as-key-audience-and-controller-of-thoughts is missed out of the analysis altogether!

When talking with someone in conversation, however, the resonance metaphor (transmission/receiver tower) also suggests that you will have multiple other resonances happening other than just talking with the person in front of you. Most go 'unnoticed' (not preparing for talking out loud) but some we do notice. Now because this is not a particle-conflict-billiard-balls-colliding metaphor, the strong resonance of these other thoughts does not imply that you do not like the person in front of you or are bored by their conversation, although people sometimes feel guilty about this. It does tell us, however, that those other thoughts are important in our social strategies, whether good or bad. There are multiple thoughts from our multiple audiences (who do not have to be there), but they are not fighting for cognitive processing space!

Historically, in a person's life, parents and siblings are key people who probably shape a lot of how we think and what becomes verbally rehearsed material or not. Freud recognized this and wrote of the conscious and unconscious thoughts as being shaped by ego (Mead's social self) and the superego. The latter seems to be a mixture of parents and generalized other, as he also hinted that it is close to what we mean by a *conscience*, but in Freud's day the parents – and father in particular – played a dominant role as the 'face' of any generalized other. Today this generalized other would be based more on media characters and pop culture references than parents.

When we are day-dreaming we might not have any but a 'generalized other' as our contextualizing audience, as we saw earlier described by sociologists Cooley and Mead. Most often, however, there are some 'pressing matters' or important outcomes about which we day-dream thoughts. Freud suggested that the people who are relevant to 'fulfilling our sexual needs' determine a large part of our background thinking, even if, as we will see later in this chapter, 'we' might disguise any of these thoughts that could get verbally rehearsed.

In essence, any of the audiences that control our other behaviors can and will control our thinking. They will not 'control' our thoughts like some sort of mind control, but they will influence us like multiple waves resonating attuned organisms, in the range and diversity of thinklings amongst all the other audiences and contexts that are also resonating at any time. A lot will therefore revolve around the historical context of what has been heard, spoken, and thought in the past, and what interests, consequences, or resources are contingent on any action.

To get a feel for this, think of a time when you perhaps heard someone you did not know at all speak forcibly about an issue. You might have been for or against the issue, it does not matter, but afterwards you are likely to find yourself rethinking some of the same ideas, or coming up with counter-arguments, or thinking good or bad thoughts about that person. This suggests how that particular new audience has influenced the range and diversity of your thoughts, but they are not 'taking over your thoughts' in a mind-control fashion as in SF movies. You still have a multiplicity of thoughts occurring from many audiences, but the balance has been changed a little.

However, we must approach this carefully. Not everyone whom you hear speak affects you in this way, so we still need to analyze and understand why in some contexts people affect our future thinklings and not in others. This goes back to the main points above and below, that this will occur when there are important resource interests or stakes, where there are bad outcomes from people (not necessarily the person who is affecting our thinking), and where there are conflicts which have real outcomes (Guerin, forthcoming; Rose, 1998).

Ultimately, talking to oneself is from economic, social, cultural, historical, and environmental contexts

Picking up on a point from the last section, ultimately thoughts will depend upon all the normal contexts that resonate our behavior – social, cultural, historical, economic, etc. (Guerin, 2004, forthcoming). As we saw in earlier chapters, this does require a certain way of observing to 'see' these contexts – what I have earlier called *contextual observation*. The same applies to thinking and talking-to-oneself.

This book has considered it unfruitful to think about thinking as something occurring in isolation from social relationships and other contexts. That is like trying to find a 'gravity entity' inside the Earth which controls gravity independently of the other bodies in the solar system: like a cognitive processing center it would compute where all the planets are and enforce the right amount of pull and attraction once it made its decisions.

This approach, therefore, interestingly allows for analyzing how all sorts of contexts change or determine our thinking. We can therefore have an analysis of how economic contexts and pressures influence thinking and talking about oneself, how different types of social relationships allow different ranges of background and 'conscious' thoughts. People belonging to different strata of society or cultures will have different opportunities for thinking in different ways with this approach. This opens up some really interesting research and new ideas to make some of these loose ideas – like culturally different thinking – more realistic and concrete so as to observe and document them more systematically.

The social strategies of cognitive models

There is not the space to go into much detail about the vast range of cognitive models of thinking and how they fit (or not) with the new metaphors. In general they have an internal focus in which representations of the world are made and 'processed' to give us our decisions and hence our actions through internal control. Some of these points were criticized in Chapter 1 of this book, and elsewhere (Potter & Edwards, 2003).

Most of these models rely on what I call 'professional acquiescence' to the following:

- metaphors of 'deep' and 'inner';
- people must let out traumatic feelings to catharsize;
- people cannot stand uncertainty or ambiguity and must resolve these;
- self-talk is an inner, private thing.

Like most psychology models, they are trying to drive the human system from within or at least with an internal agency (Guerin, 2001a, 2001b). The outside is taken 'inside' and then that is where all the behavior is driven. There are two major ways this maneuver has been performed in cognitive models. I will go through them a little because it is instructive to see how these metaphors force us to think in certain ways. Going through these also helps, I think, to get a feel for the new metaphors in this book.

Cognitive consistency models. Cognitive consistency models drive the thought-system by suggesting that if there are inconsistent or contradictory thoughts, especially with people's reports of their beliefs and attitudes, then the thinking system works by trying to resolve the inconsistency (Feldman, 1966). This can be done by changing other thoughts, or by creating new thoughts to discredit older ones. So our thinking is a mix of detecting contradictions and resolving them through (internal) decisions of change. This is clearly a conflicting-particle metaphor.

For example, I might hear a good friend say they are positive on an issue about which I am extremely negative. The 'cognitive dissonance', as it has been called, arising from this contradiction leads my cognitive processes to probably change either my attitude towards my friend or else my attitude towards the issue in question. There are other possibilities, little discussed usually: that I could stop thinking about issues at all; I could drug myself so I do not have to think; or I could find a discursive way out such as changing my 'self-image' to highlight that I am a person of 'great tolerance' who does not judge friends by their views. We also sometimes resolve these in the short term by a rhetorical strategy of "We agree to disagree on this issue." So note already that when thinking is put as an external social strategy metaphor, as I am doing here, there are many external strategies that are ignored in the academic literature.

I have argued elsewhere (Guerin 2001b) that the contradictions and dissonance might be real, but they are out there in our relationships and their resources outcomes, not inside our heads – they are contradictions and conflicts between our audiences and the contexts we have with our audiences, not something inside us. We only feel 'dissonant' when something of social importance occurs (involving resource outcomes). There are thousands of contradictions in life (to be strict, when talking about life), but most do not surface or resonate because there are no consequences. People can hold on to glaring contradictions if they have other discursive strategies in place (Potter & Wetherell, 1988): "Yes, I know my behavior seems at odds, but God has told me to do this." Thus *'cognitive dissonance' is really 'social dissonance'* and exists externally, not inside our heads.

For example, I know my good friend does not believe in abortion because of other beliefs they propound, whereas I am generally supportive of pro-choice. Here is a glaring contradiction, but we still go on being friends. So when does this become a situation of 'cognitive dissonance'? Is it always hidden in the background, causing me angst? I suggest that it only becomes a problem when the external context makes it important: my friend and I are walking and come across a pro- or anti-abortion rally. That is when the contradiction is apparent. It is only when my audience is in external conflict, not from some inner cognitive dissonance.

It is also the case, as mentioned above, that life and our talking have thousands of contradictions. If I am pro-choice that does not mean I only and exclusively know statements and arguments in favor of pro-choice. I also know all the arguments against pro-choice. So do they all sit in the background of my 'inner mind' and fight all the time with intense dissonance? How do I sleep at night? Rather, there is only a problem when external contexts make a problem. This is therefore, I argue, better thought of with a resonant waves metaphor, where there does not have to be conflict.

A more telling critique, however, going back to Chapter 3, is that contradictions do not exist in any case, except in how we speak about things and events to others and (now) to ourselves. We can have real conflicts of interest involving resource outcomes, such as what my friend might do if they know I am strongly against their view, but the contradictions themselves are not a problem because they exist only in words. *'Cognitive' contradictions are really social differences between our different audiences.*

In this sense, inconsistent thoughts are prevalent and merely reflect that our thoughts follow (resonate from) our involvement with different people and resources as outcomes of our behaviors, and that there are always resource conflicts resonating through us. In fact, inconsistent thoughts are sometimes called 'cognitive polyphasia', but I am suggesting they are common. It is the *expression* of the contradictory thoughts that is uncommon and that will depend upon the social (and cultural) context at any time (Wagner, Duveen, Verma, & Themel, 2000). The real (social) dissonance comes when my friend asks me to say out loud (commit to outcomes) what I think about abortion.

Finally, there is a point that follows from the discussion in Chapter 3 about rhetoric and discursive analyses, which can be applied now to consistency in talk: why should consistency in talking be a problem at all; what makes people want to be consistent (if they do)? It was suggested that most consistency is about consistency between different uses of language and that people try to be consistent when it is a useful discursive strategy, not by some instinct or principle of linguistic form. If contradictions only exist in words anyway, then contradictions should not be a problem.

The point about discursive strategies is that most often we get more done with our uses of language if we speak in consistent ways – we have more impact on whatever is being done through language use. There are exceptions, as with all discursive strategies. For beguiling an audience to see me as a wise guru and do what I command, I can strategically make use of contradictions and inconsistencies: "I am both the greatest and least of you all. I am the Sea and I am not the Sea. To hear me is to see me and to see me is to hear me." You probably know this sort of talk. So once you overcome the metaphors that such talk reflects or represents your self, they can be seen as often quite powerful discursive strategies.

It has also been argued that even purely logical thinking, the most consistent of all, is shaped by social conversational strategies, although more space would be needed to make this argument (Bentley, 1932, 1945; Dewey, 1938; Guerin, 2004). If the reader can think, as suggested above, that consistency is a social phenomenon (Guerin, 1994, 2004; Lin, 2001), that if we are consistent (in our talk) it is because this is shaped by other people and not by the rest of the world, then he or she can begin to appreciate that even the use of logical calculus is socially controlled. There is nothing that constrains us to be consistent in our talk (other than audiences), and in some ways consistency can even be thought of as a negative thing: the environment is always changing, so to be consistent in all contexts might be maladaptive. But, as suggested earlier, consistency is about the stories and explanations we give and is the only real alternative to monitoring people when we cannot see what they are talking about. If someone says she or he has a headache, we cannot check on that; however, we can check the consistency of what the person says over time to find out if she or he is saying it just to avoid something rather than having a 'real' headache. Mentalistic language is a (social) rhetorical method for secrecy and avoiding consequences.

Logical thinking, therefore, can be seen as a special conversational strategy in which a context is set up for getting agreement from listeners about assumptions (the logical premises) that will then constrain future talking about behavior if the person is to show consistency. But getting the agreement of those assumptions in the first place is the most critical part of winning with logic, and this is clearly about social influence, social control, and establishing 'facts' (Dewey, 1938; Edwards, 1991, 1997). Making the person want to show consistency is already built into most social situations, for reasons given earlier. There is even evidence that some people consider using logical arguments with friends to be rude (Guerin, 1995), meaning that there are social contexts for being 'logical' or not. So the most 'rational' of all individualistic language use, logic itself, is controlled within social contexts and is not a social-neutral structure given to us by the world (Bentley, 1932; Dewey, 1938).

Uncertainty reduction models. The second underlying metaphor of cognitive models, widespread but rarely examined (Guerin, 2001b), is that of uncertainty reduction. Like cognitive consistency, this is also used theoretically to drive an agentive internal 'mind' or 'self', and occurs in many places and in many guises, from Freud to cognitive-processing metaphors. The basic idea is to say that the world is too much for people to handle so people simplify and reduce the world to more simple units. For the contextual approach, this really only refers to the idea that people use (simple) words a lot. Without words we can actually deal with all sorts of system complexities and chaos, but when dealing with the world through words, things need to be simplified. That is, the problem of needing to simplify our complex worlds only ever arises when we need to talk to someone about things.

There are two main forms of this metaphor that have been made. First, it is said that the uncertainty about what is true or not in the world, or the uncertainty about the ultimate meaning and outcomes of life (in the religious case usually), is too stressful or difficult to deal with so people simplify in order to cope. The second form of this argument is that there is too much information out there to process and make decisions about and so people's cognitive processing must simplify and deal with this in approximate or heuristic ways (Guerin, 1998, 2001b).

Like with cognitive consistency, I think the answer to these views is that having uncertainty or complexity in the world is not a problem unless there are conflicts with relationships leading to outcomes (consequences), and this is especially so when we have to speak of them and commit to real outcomes. There are thousands of things that are uncertain but we do not panic over them; I do not know how big this file is that I am writing, but I do not go into a panic over that. But the question really is one of: what situations are there that we get overwhelmed by; when would I get panicky over the number of words in this file? These again are typically contexts that involve other people close to us and those involved in our real outcomes. The sources are therefore external and are really only a problem for anxiety when put into words. They are not an inner source of angst driving us to do and think everything.

Without giving more details of the critique (Guerin, 2001b), the point for the present discussion is that cognitive models based on uncertainty reduction as their 'driver' (which is most of them) go on to explain our thinking in terms of biased, over-simplified, or just plain faulty thinking about the external world, and that this occurs because we have had to simplify and distort when turning the external world into thoughts which are processed, which then leads to action.

Ironically, many of the strategies thus produced in cognitive psychology are similar to those of Freud, especially as written in his case-studies, but for Freud the 'drivers' come from repressed unconscious wishes, desires, or instincts (which have simplified our worlds) finding their way out so as to be expressed or *catharsized*. The same events occur for cognitive psychology because the external world has been simplified and processing does not match 'reality'. In fact, this is not really ironic because both are wrapping the same metaphors around the same basic observations of what people do and what they report their thoughts to be, so it actually should be no surprise they are attempting to account for similar outcomes but with very different theoretical apparatuses.

Conversational strategies in thoughts and thinking

We can learn something about the strategies of thinking from extrapolating the main thrust of this chapter – that thinking is contextually driven in the same way as other language uses, such as talking and writing: it is not altogether special nor confined to an 'inner' person. What this means is that *we should expect all of the conversational language strategies to appear in thinking* as well, perhaps slightly modified, though. All the strategic maneuvers of conversation and rhetoric can therefore appear in thinking, since it is just like a quiet version of social conversation with absent or generalized audiences but driven in the same way. We have seen a couple of examples of this already.

There is not the space here to go through a review of conversational strategies (Guerin, 2003, 2004, forthcoming). Some main categories, however, are:

(1) using language to build and maintain social relationships;
(2) persuading people by using details and vivid imagery;
(3) persuading people by using categories;
(4) persuading people by using arguments and accounts;
(5) getting people to do things with directives;
(6) using extremes to enhance agreement from the listener;
(7) using hedging and mitigation to lessen the impact of consequences for what is said;
(8) using hedging, lying, and obfuscation to keep secrets from listeners or to disguise;
(9) using politeness to get more agreement;
(10) challenging or criticizing the above strategies when used by others.

What is being said is that when analyzing thinking and the contexts that bring thinking about, these conversational strategies should all appear. We have seen indications through this book, and this chapter in particular, of people's thinking certainly involving (2), (4), (5), and (10). People ruminate about criticizing and complaining about other people. People talk to themselves as though they are giving themselves directives, which we saw earlier does not guarantee obedience to those directives; which is just the same for giving directives to other people in conversation ("You should stop eating chocolates so much" compared to "I should stop eating chocolates so much"). Without the right social contexts in place neither of these is likely to take place – telling yourself to do things has no 'inner' authority for obedience, just as the words you use to tell someone else to stop eating chocolates have no 'inner' authority to work! Both only have power to do something through social strategies and relationships.

Strategies (7) and (8) are interesting cases, and I will say more about them below when talking of Freud's mechanism of 'repression' and a wonderful discursive analysis version of this by Michael Billig. For strategy (1), we would seem to rehearse a lot of jokes, stories, and other relationship-building talk as resonating thoughts, and we sometimes laugh at the things we think. When engaged in conversation we are trained to resonate thoughts that will produce more jokes and good conversation. They just appear to us, even though some should be edited.

I will not go through all these, especially since the real work of researching them is yet to be done. What I will do is look at a few other schemes for analyzing thoughts and show how they can be subsumed as examples of the above conversational strategies applied to thinking and thoughts.

For strategy (3), a lot of the category use in conversation is about strategically talking about yourself for self-presentational reasons, and self-image building for social relationships and hence resources. Examples can be simple, such as "I often think that my way of doing things sheds more light on these questions," or highly involved, such as "I think I am the sort of person who examines the evidence first before jumping in with crass solutions." These are using categories to build image management strategies. This means that the act of talking (as if) to oneself can itself be utilized in later conversations for image management:

- "I pray to myself a lot."
- "As you can see, I have been thinking about this a lot."
- "I'm a deep, meditative person."
- "I just need to think about that for a bit" (stalling).

What is being argued here, however, is that the effect of these is on other people, not on some hidden inner 'me'. I resonate or think these because they are the sorts of words that have been rehearsed in the past to impress other people in a certain way. My self-image is a product, once again, of my external contexts and especially my social relationships. And with multiple audiences come multiple images of self.

Discursive strategies implicit in psychotherapies

Some systems of psychotherapy implicitly analyze conversational or discursive strategies in both what people say in therapy and in their thinking. Indeed, this is characteristic of the modern cognitive therapy movement – that how we think and talk about ourselves, people, and the world can be wrong and lead to serious problems in life. If I think of myself as 'fat', then this can affect my other behaviors badly. These models follow the cognitive metaphors, obviously, so the strategies are said to result from faulty cognitive processing or decision making when we try and simplify the world, but the same points can be seen to be derived from conversational strategies.

As our example, one of the founders of cognitive behavior therapy, Aaron Beck (1976), suggested on the basis of his clinical experience that the following faulty modes of cognitive information processing lead to clinical disorders:

- arbitrary inference
- selective abstraction
- overgeneralization
- magnification and minimization
- personalization
- dichotomous thinking
- ignoring the positive.

I will not go through all these, but what is being said here is that we can forgo the cognitive metaphor and think instead that these are typical strategies which are used in conversation in social context, and they also occur in thinking 'conversations' and lead to problematic outcomes. For example, a really useful conversational strategy which can easily be defended if challenged is that of using dichotomous categories to persuade a listener: "Men and women are just different, Bruce. Look around you at the men and women you see." Similar points have been made by others, although they often take this as evidence of primitive models of thought or hard-wired modes of thought when it is really a social property of easily convincing a listener and defending against challenges (Lévi-Strauss, 1966).

So the point is that we do not have to treat these strategies as faulty cognitive processing but as examples of the typical conversational strategies we use in everyday life but applied to our own thinking resonances. When applied to talking and thinking about ourselves and our relationships, however, they can make things go wrong. But they are 'out there' in our external worlds rather than 'in here' as faulty or distorted cognitions. So 'ignoring the positive' and 'selective abstraction' are quite functional in other arenas of our social life, and that is where they resonate from.

A very different version comes from Bandler and Grinder (1975a, 1975b), who examined masters of therapy to find their strategies, people such as Milton H. Erickson. Grinder was himself a linguist by training, so it is no coincidence they saw grammatical patterns, although I am translating these into pragmatics here rather than transformational grammar, as they did. One of their schemes highlighted how clients in therapy often produce *generalizations, deletions of grammatical referents*, and *distortions* (pp. 57ff.). Similarities can be seen with some of Beck's categories, above. They took the next step of suggesting new forms of therapy where the language itself was used as a basis for changing the clients' ways of talking. The same can be applied, of course, to clients' thoughts and thinking using the material from this chapter. A later version (1975b, p. 157) had strategies of nominalization, selectional restrictions, ambiguity, embedded questions, embedded commands, and derived meanings.

Types of unconscious editing

We have already seen some of Freud's view on thinking and the unconscious. He saw that there were always many thoughts that popped out of the context (thinklings), some of them being rehearsed or prepared to say ('conscious'), but most not ('unconscious'). He saw there being conflicts and anxieties in some of the thoughts that resonate from contexts although he placed all this as going on inside the head of a person rather than the conflicts being outside in the diverse external contexts. He also, for reasons to do with his clients' talking and perhaps his era, saw conflicts mainly as arising over sexuality and desire/love. His system also had the conscious ego editing and doing work to any thinking that popped up, and solving battles between desires and wants (I would say outside resources). The desires were called the id (an invented English word, whereas sticking to Nietzsche's 'it' might have been better since that is also the German word Freud used), and the sum of pressure to conform called the superego (heavily represented by fathers and society, the two major influences on people in his day). In certain situations, mainly slips of the tongue, dreams, day-dreams, and when freely associating words, the unconscious would disguise or edit what was being thought unconsciously where there was conflict – present or incipient.

What Freud was saying, then, was that the background unconscious thoughts were edited and some never allowed to be consciously rehearsed or made explicit. Some were of no interest and were never conscious but the ones of particular importance were those *repressed* or *edited* so they never appeared consciously to the person. He called this the 'dream work' when he was considering the analysis of dreams. His role, as analyst, was to elicit and hear from the client the allowable material and try and interpret or goad the client into thinking these repressed background thoughts. His conceptual model behind this was a strong catharsis model as we saw earlier: repressed thoughts were full of energy and this energy would 'come out' in other ways if repressed, and these ways of 'coming out' were usually the presenting symptoms of mental illness.

Put in the simplest form, Freud was saying (1915/1984, p. 175):

> [I]f, on testing, it is rejected by the censorship, it is not allowed to pass into the second phase; it is then said to be 'repressed' and must remain unconscious.

The methods for finding out these repressed thoughts were many, but psychoanalysts of all persuasions were keen to focus on the associations or free responding to the context, and what thoughts appeared. Psychoanalysts also liked dream material because thoughts reappeared that had been forgotten 'innocently', as well as the edited or 'repressed' ones.

> We instruct the patient to put himself into a state of quiet, unreflecting self-observation, and to report to us whatever internal perceptions he is able to make – feelings, thoughts memories – in the order in which they occur to him. At the same time we warn him expressly against giving way to any motive which would lead him to make a selection among these associations or to exclude any of them, whether on the ground that it is too *disagreeable* or too *indiscreet* to say, or that it is too *unimportant* or *irrelevant*, or that it is *nonsensical* and need not be said.
>
> (Freud, 1917, p. 328)

Linking these thoughts and free associations were good methods, but sometimes the enterprise went haywire because linking this back to context and resources and audiences was over-interpreted and over-theorized.

While repression was the most extensively discussed strategy of thoughts, there were others as well, from which we can learn. In Freud's works, the following ways of *editing* are mentioned (Freud, 1915/1984; Rapaport, 1951, p. 338ff., footnotes):

- censorship
- reality testing
- self-criticism
- displacement
- representation
- symbolism

- projection
- isolation
- negation
- denial
- intellectualization
- rationalization
- condensation.

We can again see the parallels with conversational and discursive strategies given earlier – strategies that are commonly used between people talking and getting each other to do and believe things. A lot of these correspond to conversational strategies labelled earlier as (7) and (8). They are typical conversational strategies when trying to hedge some consequences of talking or trying to evade or escape consequences by disguising or keeping secret.

This was put as an internal equivalent by Rapaport (1951, p. 339, Editor's footnote 2), who used inner organization as his metaphor and not the parallel with conversational strategies being suggested here:

> From the point of view of psychoanalysis, projection is first of all a defense mechanism; from the point of view of the theory of thinking, it is one of the mechanisms of thought-organization. While projection as a defense mechanism is fairly well understood, as a mechanism of thought-organization which has many variants suggesting a hierarchic layering it has not yet been systematically explored.

In conversational analysis, for example, projection is a strategy of responsibility attribution in which language strategies are used to take responsibility off the speaker (or thinker in our present case) and place responsibility on someone or something else.

Types of repression and similar strategies of thoughts

I will now focus on the main form of editing discussed by Freud, that of *repression*. This is useful because you can also read in parallel an excellent account of how repression looks when considered in a discursive or conversational analysis, and with a more detailed contextual analysis (Billig, 1997, 1998, 1999, 2006).

Earlier I gave a long case-study quotation from Sigmund Freud (1909) on intrusive thoughts. My point was that it was not the intrusiveness that was a problem ('all thoughts are intrusive') but the other social contexts in place that changed the outcome from merely dismissing such silly thoughts with a laugh to an outcome of becoming confused and sick and seriously contemplating suicide. We must remember that most of these multiple, resonating background thoughts go nowhere, even the ones we think but we would consider nasty, naughty, or not in line with who we think we are.

Freud mainly dealt with people who responded poorly to their thoughts, by becoming anxious or delusionsal about them, and he attempted to analyze some of the social context to make sense of these episodes. The thoughts themselves do not *cause* the poor reactions to thinking in a particular way – the other social contexts determine that.

Here is another example of someone who thinks (resonates to) a thought that any of us might have, quite innocently, but for which we would not deal with it, react to it, or pay much heed to it. This person clearly (she was classified as 'neurotic') had other contexts influencing her reaction (resonances, some unconscious thinklings) to what would be dismissed by most of us. The point Freud is making, and you can judge if he ends up over-stating this in his writings, is that with certain contexts in place, 'neurotics' and 'psychotics' seem to dismiss such thoughts as they have, but they actually (unconsciously) have another strategy intrude on them *to repress* that thought. Freud then looked for signs that the repressed thought had an influence in other ways that were not so obvious.

> Let me go back by way of example to a case analysed a great many years ago, in which the patient, a young woman, was in love with her brother-in-law. Standing beside her sister's death bed, she was horrified at having the thought: "Now he is free and can marry me." This scene was instantly forgotten, and thus the process of regression, which led to her hysterical pains, was set in motion. It is instructive precisely in this case, moreover, to learn along what path the neurosis attempted to solve the conflict. It took away from the value of the change that had occurred in reality, by repressing the instinctual demand which had emerged – that is, her love for her brother-in-law. The psychotic reaction would have been a disavowal of the fact of her sister's death.
>
> (Freud, 1924/1979, p. 222)

The point here is that rather than just considering that this young woman dismisses the nasty thought that resonated while at her sister's funeral, Freud sees it, with evidence to his satisfaction, as an active but unconscious strategy of repression which has later repercussions for the young woman. He goes on to link at least three strategies of our thinking:

> Or again, expressed in yet another way: neurosis does not disavow the reality, it only ignores it; psychosis disavows it and tries to replace it. We call behaviour normal or 'healthy', if it combines certain features of both reactions – if it disavows the reality as little as does a neurosis, but if it then exerts itself, as does a psychosis, to effect an alteration of that reality. Of course, this expedient, normal, behaviour leads to work being carried out on the external world; it does not stop, as in psychosis, at effecting internal changes.
> (Freud, 1924/1979, p. 224)

What we see then, for Freudian-type models (also Ellenberger, 1970; Guerin, 2001b), is that while some of these negative thoughts that resonate with us are dismissed, some for other (contextual) reasons are treated as 'active' and they 'do things'. Here is a bit of the flavor of this:

> We may construct the process on the model of a neurosis, with which we are more familiar. There we see that a reaction of anxiety sets in whenever the repressed instinct makes a thrust forward, and that the outcome of the conflict is only a compromise and does not provide complete satisfaction. Probably in a psychosis the rejected piece of reality constantly forces itself upon the mind, just as the repressed instinct does in a neurosis, and that is why in both cases the consequences too are the same. The elucidation of the various mechanisms which are designed, in the psychoses, to turn the subject away from reality and to reconstruct reality – this is a task for specialized psychiatric study which has not yet been taken in hand.
> (Freud, 1924/1979, pp. 224–225)

What we can see is that when some issue eventuates out of thinklings, while the Freudian (and other) approaches do not put a 'self' in charge of deciding and thinking with total control – that is, they do not put a *consciousness* in charge of sorting out mental matters – they still have hypothesized 'inner' agents doing the strategizing and deciding, such as the unconscious, id, or superego.

With the two cases I have set out from Freud, however, we can see that the determination of the outcomes depends on what various audiences and other contexts there are present externally. That is, we need still to look for external contexts to understand why a thought that resonates with us is not just dismissed. For most of the thoughts given in the examples above, if you or I had those thoughts it is still not that we would dismiss them, but that *we would rehearse or edit as though we were telling our friends or family and that would help us merely dismiss the thoughts*. Bringing the social control in would help.

So the point for rethinking thinking is that the contexts we are in, and the social contexts in particular, lead to thoughts and also lead to the outcomes of those thoughts happening. The question is not so much about dynamics of the unconscious repression but about why the person is repressing at all. Why for the 'neurotic' would no external social context or audience, or even just a rehearsal for one, just dismiss those thoughts, or are the clients not rehearsing or editing in the way most of us would?

One of the basic underlying 'mechanisms' of Freudian and many other psychologies is that of catharsis – that secreted, repressed, hidden, contradictory, dissonant, or other forms of dealing with conflicting thoughts merely seem to disappear but they have an energy that will continue to have effects until they have been 'released' or catharsized. This is said to 'drive' the behaviors or thoughts to continue to have an effect. There are many forms of this, for example, that if you have secretly done something wrong then it will not rest or let you be at peace until you have catharsized that deed.

Earlier I went through a number of arguments against these very basic 'driving mechanisms' of many otherwise disparate theories of psychology. The conclusion was that instead of catharsis, the situations are resolved by external contexts changing – not some inner conflict resolved by thoughts being relieved of energy (Guerin, 2001b). Dissonance theory, for example, says that if we have dissonant or contradictory thoughts then there is a drive to change something to remove this noxious state of dissonance (Festinger). Through several examples, I showed that in each case what actually changed was something to do with the audiences for those conflicting thoughts.

Note that this is not saying that the basic thinking and conflict and some form of changed behavior do not happen. What it is saying is that conceptualizing this as happening in some sort of thought-space inside a person is not tenable. We must look to external contexts – and especially social ones for the examples I have been using here – to understand what is going on and how to intervene. The woman at her sister's funeral has that thought, and the thought keeps bugging her after she outwardly dismisses it, not because of some unconscious energy which keeps it active but repressed, but because some external contexts keep resonating. This is why I say that the unconscious forces are real but they are influences from external contexts that are very real, not an 'inner world' somewhere in the body.

Another common way of dealing with this conceptualization has been to put the 'energy' that 'controls' the thoughts onto symbols. So in some analyses, that which is repressed is turned into a symbol which might be local or generalized (collective: Jung). However, from the contextual approach it must be remembered that a symbol, like the words of a language in Chapter 3, does not drive itself. If the symbolism can effect or change something in thinking it is only by way of the audiences, training, and the resources to which they provide access.

Symbols only affect us if we have other people influencing us (the second machines of the virtual surgery). That is, symbols by themselves cannot do anything to a person, unless the person treats them and rehearses them by way of a generalized other. One can rehearse a symbol and come to think of it as having a power to do something, but that is only from the generalized other and very general societal resources, if I can then influence others to go along with me.

Some similar points to the above have been argued by Billig (1997, 1998, 1999, 2006). As an expert in conversational or discursive analysis, he turned his attention to Freud's idea of repression. He showed, as I drew upon above, how instead of an inner censorship, repression is very much about conversational strategies to conceal things from real external audiences with real repercussions.

Billig is especially perceptive in delving into the case of 'Dora', whom Freud had as a client and wrote about. Without repeating everything here, Billig shows how the external social contexts – and the political contexts of how women and Jews were treated in that era – were the setting events or contexts for Dora's strange behaviors. The point being made, and these papers by Billig should be read, is that resonating thoughts emerge from external social contexts, and so does any editing, rehearsing, or changing of those thoughts like repression. Billig's work is useful because he goes into more specific details than I can do here, and about a very specific case of some importance.

How can we rethink thoughts?

Unfortunately, writing on this fascinating topic at greater length will have to wait. What I have tried to get across to readers here is that we can totally rethink the current ways of conceptualizing thoughts and thinking. This does not mean everyone before was wrong, just their ways of talking about the phenomena and, more importantly, how and where they looked to change thinking.

This chapter needs a lot of work on your part to try out the metaphors and rethinking so that you can conceptualize that 'thinking' is multiple all the time, that it is outside of us in our contexts, only some thinklings seem to us to be 'conscious' or rehearsed and edited, and that changing thinking is about changing external contexts – especially social and conversational contexts.

References

Bandler, R., & Grinder, J. (1975a). *Patterns of the hypnotic techniques of Milton H. Erickson, M.D.* (Vol. 1). Cupertino, CA: Meta Publications.

Bandler, R., & Grinder, J. (1975b). *The structure of magic I. A book about language and therapy*. Palo Alto, CA: Science and Behavior Books.

Beck, A. T. (1976). *Cognitive therapy and emotional disorders*. New York: International Universities Press.

Bentall, R. P. (2003). *Madness explained: Psychosis and human nature*. London: Allen Lane.

Bentall, R. P. (2009). *Doctoring the mind: Why psychiatric treatments fail*. London: Penguin Books.

Bentley, A. F. (1932). *Linguistic analysis of mathematics*. Bloomington, IN: Principia Press.

Bentley, A. F. (1945). On a certain vagueness in logic: 1. *Journal of Philosophy*, 42, 6–27.

Billig, M. (1997). Freud and Dora: repressing an oppressed identity. *Theory, Culture & Society*, 14, 29–55.

Billig, M. (1998). Rhetoric and the unconscious. *Argumentation*, 12, 199–216.

Billig, M. (1999). *Freudian repression: Conversation creating the unconscious*. Cambridge, UK: Cambridge University Press.

Billig, M. (2006). A psychoanalytic discursive psychology: From consciousness to unconsciousness. *Discourse Studies*, 8, 17–24.

Borch-Jacobsen, M., & Shamdasani, S. (2012). *The Freud files: An inquiry into the history of psychoanalysis*. New York: Cambridge University Press.

Buehler, K. (1951). On thought connections. In D. Rapaport (Ed.), *Organization and pathology of thought: Selected sources* (pp. 40–57). New York: Columbia University Press.

Cooley, C. H. (1902). *Human nature and the social order*. Glencoe, IL: The Free Press.

Cooley, C. H. (1909). *Social organization: A study of the larger mind*. Glencoe, IL: The Free Press.

Cushman, P. (1990). Why the self is empty: Toward a historically situated psychology. *American Psychologist*, 45, 599–611.

Deleuze, G. (1991). *Empiricism and subjectivity: An essay on Hume's theory of human nature*. New York: Columbia University Press.

Deleuze, G. (2004). *Desert islands and other texts. 1953–1974*. New York: Semiotext(e).

Dennett, D. C. (1969). *Content and consciousness*. New York: Routledge.

Dewey, J. (1938). *Logic: The theory of inquiry*. New York: Holt.

Edwards, D. (1991). Categories are for talking: On the cognitive and discursive bases of categorization. *Theory & Psychology*, 1, 515–542.

Edwards, D. (1997). *Discourse and cognition*. London: Sage.

Ellenberger, H. F. (1970). *The discovery of the unconscious: The history and evolution of dynamic psychiatry*. London: Allen Lane.

Erickson, M. H., Rossi, E. L., & Rossi, S. I. (1976). *Hypnotic realities: The induction of clinical hypnosis and forms of indirect suggestion*. New York: Irvington.

Feldman, S. (Ed.). (1966). *Cognitive consistency*. New York: Academic Press.

Festinger, L. (1954). A theory of social comparison processes. *Human Relations*, 7, 114–140.

Freud, S. (1900/1975). *The interpretation of dreams* (Penguin Freud Library Vol. 4). London: Penguin Books.

Freud, S. (1909/1979). *Notes upon a case of obsessional neurosis (the 'Rat Man')* (Penguin Freud Library Vol. 9). London: Penguin Books.

Freud, S. (1915/1984). *The unconscious* (Penguin Freud Library Vol. 11). London: Penguin Books.

Freud, S. (1917/1974). *Introductory lectures on psycho-analysis*. London: Penguin Books.

Freud, S. (1924/1979). *The loss of reality in neurosis and psychosis* (Penguin Freud Library Vol. 10). London: Penguin Books.

Gee, J. P. (1992). *The social mind: Language, ideology, and social practice*. New York: Bergin & Garvey.

Gibson, J. J. (1979). *An ecological approach to visual perception*. Boston: Houghton Mifflin.

Guerin, B. (1990). Gibson, Skinner, and perceptual responses. *Behavior and Philosophy*, 18, 43–54.

Guerin, B. (1992). Behavior analysis and the social construction of knowledge. *American Psychologist*, 47, 1423–1432.

Guerin, B. (1994). Attitudes and beliefs as verbal behavior. *Behavior Analyst*, 17, 155–163.

Guerin, B. (1995). Social influence in one-to-one and group situations: Predicting influence tactics from basic group processes. *Journal of Social Psychology*, 135, 371–385.

Guerin, B. (1998). Religious behaviors as strategies for organizing groups of people: A social contingency theory. *Behavior Analyst*, 21, 53–72.

Guerin, B. (2001a). Individuals as social relationships: 18 ways that acting alone can be thought of as social behavior. *Review of General Psychology*, 5, 406–428.

Guerin, B. (2001b). Replacing catharsis and uncertainty reduction theories with descriptions of the historical and social context. *Review of General Psychology*, 5, 44–61.

Guerin, B. (2003). Language use as social strategy: A review and an analytic framework for the social sciences. *Review of General Psychology*, 7, 251–298.

Guerin, B. (2004). *Handbook for analyzing the social strategies of everyday life*. Reno, NV: Context Press.

Guerin, B. (forthcoming). *Understanding people through social contextual analysis: A practical guide*. Abingdon: Routledge.

Guerin, B., & Miyazaki, Y. (2006). Analyzing rumors, gossip, and urban legends through their conversational properties. *Psychological Record*, 56, 23–34.

Harris, M. (1979). *Cultural materialism: The struggle for a science of culture*. New York: Random House.

Hayes, L. J. (1994). Thinking. In S. C. Hayes, L. J. Hayes, M. Sato, & K. Ono (Eds.), *Behavior analysis of language and cognition* (pp. 149–164). Reno, NV: Context Press.

Hayes, S. C., & Sackett, C. (2005). Acceptance and commitment therapy. In Michel Hersen & Johan Rosqvist (Eds.), *Encyclopedia of behavior modification and cognitive behavior therapy: Vol. 1. Adult clinical applications* (pp. 1–5). Thousand Oaks, CA: Sage Publications.

Hood, B. (2012). *The self illusion*. London: Constable.

Janet, P. (1919/1925). *Psychological healing: A historical and clinical study*. London: George Allen & Unwin.

Jones, P. E. (2009). From 'external speech' to 'inner speech' in Vygotsky: A critical appraisal and fresh perspectives. *Language & Communication*, 29, 166–181.

Josephs, I. E., & Valsiner, J. (1998). How does autodialogue work? Miracles of meaning maintenance and circumvention strategies. *Social Psychology Quarterly*, 61, 68–83.

Kantor, J. R. (1981). *Interbehavioral philosophy*. Chicago: Principia Press.

Kennedy, J. (1998). Thinking is social: Experiments with the adaptive culture model. *Journal of Conflict Resolution*, 42, 56–76.

Lévi-Strauss, C. (1966). *The savage mind*. London: Weidenfeld & Nicolson.

Lin, M. (2001). *Certainty as a social metaphor: The social and historical production of certainty in China and the West*. London: Greenwood Press.

Mead, G. H. (1934). *Mind, self, and society from the standpoint of a social behaviorist*. Chicago: University of Chicago Press.

Nietzsche, F. (1886/1966). *Beyond good and evil: Prelude to a philosophy of the future*. New York: Vintage Books.

Nietzsche, F. (1967). *The will to power*. New York: Vintage Books.

Peirce, C. S. (1955). *Philosophical writings of Peirce*. New York: Dover.

Perls, F. (1969). *Gestalt therapy verbatim*. Lafayette, CA: Real People Press.

Potter, J., & Edwards, D. (2003). Rethinking cognition: On Coulter on discourse and mind. *Human Studies*, 26, 165–181.

Potter, J., & Wetherell, M. (1988). Accomplishing attitudes: Fact and evaluation in racist discourse. *Text*, 8, 51–68.

Rapaport, D. (Ed.). (1951). *Organization and pathology of thought: Selected sources*. New York: Columbia University Press.

Rose, N. (1996). Authority and the genealogy of subjectivity. In P. Heelas, S. Lash, & P. Morris (Eds.), *Detraditionalization: Critical reflections on authority and identity* (pp. 294–327). London: Blackwell.

Rose, N. (1998). *Inventing our selves: Psychology, power, and personhood*. Cambridge, UK: Cambridge University Press.

Sampson, E. E. (1993). *Celebrating the other: A dialogic account of human nature*. Boulder, CO: Westview Press.

Sartre, J.-P. (1937/1991). *The transcendence of the ego: An existentialist theory of consciousness*. New York: Farrar, Straus, and Giroux.

Stanley, S. (2012). From discourse to awareness: Rhetoric, mindfulness, and a psychology without foundations. *Theory & Psychology*, 23, 60–80.

Stekel, W. (1951, orig. 1924). The polyphony of thought. In D. Rapaport (Ed.), *Organization and pathology of thought: Selected sources* (pp. 311–314). New York: Columbia University Press.

Suzuki, D. T. (1969). *The Zen doctrine of no mind*. London: Rider & Co.

Wagner, W., Duveen, G., Verma, J., & Themel, M. (2000). 'I have some faith and at the same time I don't believe' – cognitive polyphasia and cultural change in India. *Journal of Community and Applied Social Psychology*, 10, 301–314.

Watson, J. B. (1924). *Behaviorism*. New York: Norton.

Wertsch, J. V. (1985). *Vygotsky and the social formation of mind*. London: Harvard University Press.

Wittgenstein, L. (1958). *Philosophical investigations*. Oxford: Basil Blackwell.

5 The Zen of running our lives

Doing, thinking, and talking

Summary of the plot so far

Let us recap and see where we have got to; recall the plot before we lose it. First, while these were given in Chapter 1, I will show again the list of metaphors and virtual realities. It would be useful to go through and make sure you remember these and still have a gut feeling for them and what they mean for our rethinking psychology.

As I wrote at the very beginning, each of these by itself does not amount to much, and if you accept all your current assumptions about understanding people, you can dispute any of these. The power of these metaphors comes from first, using them and getting a real sense of what they do to change your thinking, and second, putting them all together so all your old assumptions are changed and these metaphors each then support each other for a total rethink.

Summary description of life

Let me now summarize where all these metaphors have led us, in the form of a free-outlining summary of all the points so far when describing our life. This has usually been described as our 'psychology' but the term is less assured when it becomes concrete and not about hidden or private 'minds', 'consciousnesses', or 'psyches'.

We are born within constraints and contexts not of our making. We wander around and engage in the world mainly through other people. While our principal strategies involve achieving the resources we need, by far the majority of these work through our social relationships, even with strangers, which is why so much time is spent engaging and maintaining relationships (and most of the things we 'want' are to perpetuate these relationships rather than to consume). Few of us engage directly with the non-social environment for our resources – except maybe a

Table 5.1 Metaphors that were presented in this book

Chapter	*Metaphors*
1. Understanding our own psychology	• Our actions are like lumps of Plasticine • Contexts not causes for growing seeds into plants • Contextual observations of holistic elephants
2. The ubiquitous social	• Understanding people is better thought of as attuned responding to external contexts using wave-thinking • We can utilize gravity even if physicists do not understand how it works • Attunement can be thought of as sympathetic resonance
3. Language as the original virtual reality	• Language use as the original virtual reality • Language better thought of as attuned responses to waves than as reactions to particles • Getting hit 100 percent by a brick and other brute facts of life
4. Thinking, self-talk, and how to read minds	• Thinking can also be reimagined as virtual reality • Thoughts as effects of waves rather than emitted particles

vegetable garden, although these can be for socially creating an identity rather than eating vegetables.

We encounter things and people and every encounter changes or shapes us so we are immediately different and therefore will respond differently immediately. Most of these changes are minor and not really noticeable, while other changes are complex. There are typically multiple actions that resonate – doing things, talking to people, and 'thinking' things. The latter consists of potential talking-to-people actions. Some of these, depending upon the context – rather than any internal events – get rehearsed as if they will be said.

Once we have such a history then we can be said to be attuned to engage with those events and people in new ways, and all these resonances can occur regardless of whether there is any 'stimulus' or 'trigger' in our current environment. To put this another way, our 'current environment' is not the micro-physics of what is around us but the affordances or resonances available, and this can be across time (history) and distance. Whether they resonate depends on events not necessarily present in front of us: their importance, the social relationships, their relative importance, their speakability, etc. For example, we might not do some action until what we are about to do can be spoken of or verbally defended with reasons, excuses, etc.

In all the above, therefore, actions (overt, talking, thinking) happen depending upon the external contexts and our attuned resonances. Our talking does not control our actions – they are actions that influence other people. Our thinking also does not control our actions – they are resonances that can be rehearsed or edited for influencing other people. There is no 'inner' control or executive center controlling our actions – it is the attunements from past interactions and how they resonate to things, events, and people around us. Further, when there are resonances then they occur instantaneously and fully – there are no probabilities in this, and there is no 'inner' sequential development of control. Resonances can occur in the absence of the thing or event, and they can happen at a distance, and without any things (particles) necessarily being seen to occur in the space or time between.

In all this, we do not need to worry about how this resonance and attunement take place. That will be for future generations of neuroscientists and physicists to figure out when we know better what it actually is that needs to be accounted for and how to better include the context into brain accounts. Our real goal is to learn and describe all the contexts and past contexts if we wish to understand why people do what they do, and how we might best change them when ethically appropriate.

In all this, the most frequent resonances are those attuned to social contexts. That is, the most frequent actions, conversations, and thoughts are about people or involve people. The environment principally affords talking and thinking about things, a point Gibson missed. This is the social constructionist point – that our main environment is about talking about things and events rather than acting directly on them (although acting in relation to people is actually acting directly on the environment). This arises because almost everything we do and obtain as resources comes through relationships with other people, even if strangers.

Two short examples

There are always multiple resonances for the things, events, and people we engage with in our lives. If I were to hand you right now a cricket bat then there are multiple events you could find yourself (1) doing, (2) saying to me, and (3) thinking. Working backwards, there would be many resonating *thoughts*, along the lines of: "What is this?"; "Don't want to look stupid"; "I broke my brother's bat and never told him years ago"; "What are they expecting me to do?"; jokes; stories of this incident you will tell after you leave, "So they out of the blue gave me this cricket bat. I mean it was so dumb, what did they expect me to do with it? Eat it? Haa haa"; each of these seemingly addressed to different past, future, or generalized audiences. You would also be likely *to say* a number of things, along the lines of: "That's a cricket bat, isn't it?"; "What are you giving me that for?"; "A cricket bat!"; "Haa haa! I remember once when I was younger, my brother had his very special cricket bat. Well, one day I took it out the back of our house to knock some oranges off our tree ..." You would also be likely *to do* a number of things, along the lines of: handle it; practice swinging it; pretend as a joke to hit someone or something with it; not touch it when offered; use as an air guitar.

While this is a trivial example, the doing, saying, and thinking are all arising through contexts involving past and present social relationships, and the resources that come from those relationships. From our metaphors:

- You are changed by all this (in a minor way, unless something more pathological is involved in your history!) – Plasticine.
- We do not have specify every stimulus or particle hitting the eye in order to understand your responding – gravity.
- There are many contexts involved in each of these examples and no one cause – growing seeds.
- Other people are essentially involved in all the examples given – Chapter 2.
- The talking and thinking always involve other people – original virtual reality, the second machine.
- The actions, talk, and thinking arise as resonance rather than colliding particles – sympathetic resonance.
- There are multiple concurrent resonances – waves rather than particles.
- The resonances do not conflict – attuned resonance of waves.
- All these multiple events that resonate are not controlled by an inner control center, they are controlled by external (including historical changes) contexts – waves, not particles.
- The 'source' of the sympathetic resonance does not have to be present, it could be far away or a historical change – waves rather than particles.
- To find the sources, relationships, and resources involved so that we can understand the strategic nature of each response, we would need intensive and contextual observations over time – holistic elephants.
- None of this is probabilistic but occurs 100 percent, although there are limitations of observation and documentation – getting hit by bricks.

In past psychology and common sense there has been an overemphasis on the *doing* responses (overt behavior) rather than talking, in that perception has not studied how talking and thinking are very common responses to objects (it assumes that you must be able to name the object and handle it before you can talk about it). There has also been an overemphasis on what is immediately present in the environment, and the micro-physics of those objects, rather than what has happened over time and space. There has also been an overemphasis on understanding what is happening in the immediate present rather than how all the events (including 'perception', etc.) are part of larger strategic contexts in people's lives – it has been wrongly assumed, following Descartes, that if we just figure out the immediate bits we can add them together to understand the whole.

Let me now give another example to help, from a different perspective, although I will not name all the metaphors and rethinkings this time. For this, you are a counselor, friend, or advisor, talking to someone who seems in distress. You do not know them very well, but you wish to understand their position, their predicament, and help them look for solutions. The person says to you:

> "You know, when I seriously look at myself and what I am doing in life, I really do not like myself at all. I do not like what I have become."

Commonly the thinking would be that this person 'has' or 'possesses' a negative core belief about themselves that is interfering in their life, probably through distorted cognitive processing of information they have stored in a memory deposit somewhere inside their head about their life. The goal is to change their way of talking to themselves so their other behaviors change, by changing their cognitive processing.

From the new ways of thinking, these are the questions that could be asked:

- What could be the possible (since we are not researching the person with contextual observations) contexts for this statement?
- How does this statement fit into the person's life strategically, in terms of resources and social relationships? What is it doing?
- Who might have been audiences for this sort of talking before?
- Have they said it out loud before?
- What has this sort of talk done for the person previously? What have listeners done?

- They will be having many other thoughts and background resonances; what are they?
- They will also have other opposite thoughts and background resonances, so what are their contexts and why are they not being said?
- Who are the past and present audiences of those other thoughts and background resonances?
- What are all the strategic discursive elements doing or what have they done in the past? (Elements from the quotation above include: *You know*; *seriously*; *look at myself*; *doing in life* [abstraction]; *like*; *at all* [a linguistic extreme]; *I really*.)
- Who has previously shaped these rhetorics?
- What other thinklings is the person 'not aware' of, perhaps?
- What are all their contexts that might be relevant (social, economic, cultural, historical, life opportunities)?
- What are the other thoughts, talking, and actions this person is doing?
- Are the other thoughts, talking, and actions this person is doing contradictory; if so, who are or have been the audiences for those?
- Are there other background thoughts that appear in dreams, imaginings, free associating, loose chatting, that might be of interest?

Many of these questions are commonly used in practice, but many do not follow from current metaphors of how people think and talk.

Life, words, and Zen

One of the most difficult changes to grapple with in my metaphors is the non-controlling status of the words we learn – both talking and thinking. This is so ingrained that it is hard to break from it; it seems certain that we do things because we think we must do them.

This has led to many people (Freud) and training masters (Zen) noticing strange gaps between our talk and our doing the things said:

> If we ask ourselves what is it that gives the character of strangeness to the substitutive formation and the symptom of schizophrenia, we eventually come to realize that it is the pre-dominance of what has to do with words over what has to do with things.
>
> (Freud, 1915/1984)

> A Zen student told Ummon: "Brilliancy of Buddha illuminates the whole universe."

> Before he finished the phrase Ummon asked: "You are reciting another's poem, are you not?"
> "Yes," answered the student.
> "You are sidetracked," said Ummon.
>
> (Reps, 1957, pp. 123–124)

I believe it is important to be thinking differently about these, since the major problems and issues in life usually come from two sources:

- we just cannot get the resources and relationships we strategize, no matter what we do (often social work looks after this);
- our thinklings and talking cause us distress by leading to virtual strategies that do not work as do-able strategies (psychology and Zen Buddhism look after this).

One is about problems and issues to do with getting what we want (or think we want), and getting rid of other difficulties; the second is about myriad ways that thinking and talking get us into problems, whether real or not. While this sounds simple, the realities are convoluted and complex and very delicate to sort out. My belief is that rethinking these in terms of external contexts, mainly social relationships, will help us find solutions. Metaphoring them as internal cognitive structures will not help as much, I believe.

As mentioned earlier in the book, psychology has been a historical dumping ground for events for which it is difficult to see all the external controls happening, so it has led to the proliferation of 'internal' entities and postulated 'things', and treating words as controlling what we do. This is not the fault of psychologists, since most other conceptualizations fare no better, and things go wrong with talking and thinking precisely in cases where it is unclear what is going on 'for real'. It does mean that we must be careful, because a large part of life and its issues is about dealing with these 'unnamed' resonances, which does not mean some amorphous, bad dark matter but is about those bits we cannot name (Adams & Lloyd, 1983). For example, most of psychology, and especially cognition, is about how we interact with things and events we can name. But life is not like that:

> Beware! The mind of the believer stagnates. It fails to grow outward into an unlimited, infinite universe .... By your belief in granular singularities, you deny all movement. Belief fixes a granular universe and causes that universe to persist. Nothing can be allowed to

> change because that way your non-moving universe vanishes. But it moves of itself when you do not.
>
> (Herbert, 1984)

Events surprise us because they are not things we name, or even *can* name – we cannot 'cognize' them but they happen anyway. This applies to all life, not just objects. It includes things and events about relationships, emotions, our own behavior and how we talk about them, as well as things around us. We therefore tend to overemphasize the bits that can be named (the root of many 'cognitive biases').

There are several ways of rethinking the supposed controlling nature of words in talking and thinking. I have tried to do it here by using metaphors of the second virtual reality machine (which is other people) and resonance of waves to stop thinking in terms of particles. But many other ways exist, and I will say a little more about how Zen Buddhism (or some varieties of that) tries to achieve the same goal – to get us away from relying on words as having the power to change the world and ourselves directly, rather than through people. We cannot usually just do this by ignoring words and thinking, either.

I think of this as a 'Zen of life' because there is a way of thinking about the world and acting in the world that includes the world itself in a meaningful way as part of who we are, but does not let our words about the world, life, and who we are interfere with that thinking. The latter for me is the main role of Zen and many recent therapies: to wipe out the pre-eminent role of words when we think and act in this world.

> Shuzan held out his short staff and said: "If you call this a short staff, you oppose its reality. If you do not call it a short staff, you ignore the fact. Now what do you wish to call this?"
>
> (Reps, 1957, p. 127)

And similarly to mock the words we use for self-talk and identity:

> Zuigan called out to himself every day: "Master."
> Then he answered himself: "Yes, sir."
> And after that he added: "Become sober."
> Again he answered: "Yes, sir."
> "And after that," he continued, "do not be deceived by others."
> "Yes, sir; yes, sir," he answered.
>
> (Reps, 1957, p. 104)

Zen is about changing the control of what we do by words – especially thinking that we can control our own behavior by our own talking to ourselves. Most people and therapies try to do this by introducing more words – either your own plans and hopes or those of your guide. There are many ways of doing this better that reflect the different Zen and Dao procedures – meditation, stopping words altogether, humble living, etc. However, even having said this much is misleading in that the words are still trying to control. You must learn it other than by talking to yourself.

Where to from here?

Having summarized a little, I want to finish off by outlining some of what we need next. One part is to draw out the practical process of analyzing all this rethinking of human behavior, and the second part is to put into a more understandable format how this rethinking fits with prior thinking and philosophy.

Practical methods of research, understanding, and change

The new metaphors might be fine, but can we do anything practical with it all? For me the answer is yes, because I would not bother with just rethinking if it did not lead to anything more useful. However, I will not say very much here since there is too much to go through and I have dealt with it at greater length elsewhere (Guerin, forthcoming). What I would like to do is to merely point out where things might be a little different if the metaphors send you soaring to new heights.

To understand people with these metaphors is to understand people in their external environments, as part of those environments. More like an ecology of sorts than a physics (although my belief is that physics is actually changing into an ecological science by taking the contexts for physical events far more seriously than 'particles-in-isolation'). We have large repertoires with long histories, and they all absolutely involve other people – whether close family, friends, or strangers.

What this means is that we must observe and document the contexts for human events far more than we do at present, and stop using named, hypothetical causes as substitutes for the hard work of careful and time-consuming observation. We must treat actions, talking, and thinking in the same way as having the same external contextual controls, but their properties are different and what we do with them is therefore different.

The main point is that to study human behavior in context we need to think back to the holistic elephants in Chapter 1. Our practical job will be to find ways to contextually observe and describe the different contexts in which people's different actions emerge. This is not easy, and the reader should recall the number of times I have emphasized the complexities and historical embeddedness of contexts, the convoluted social strategies weaving resources through our relationships, and the common secrecy and ways the contexts were hidden from simple observation. Our methodologies must therefore also change dramatically, and psychology should look to the methods of anthropology and some sociology a lot more.

Philosophy: on being very clear that actions, thinklings, and spoken words are not metaphysically, philosophically, or essentially different

The final thing I wish to do in this book is to put the more philosophical conceptualizations into context. This rests heavily on Chapters 2 and 3 and being clear that language is a specialized form of action that only works through other people (Chapter 3), and that talking to ourselves as if others were listening is just an extension of this (Chapter 4). I will also rely on the brute facts argument from Chapter 3. In particular, a major problem with past Western philosophy has been forgetting or ignoring that the real-world (social) link between saying words and the reality of people's reactions is what allows the abstract and wild ideas about behavior and language to raise their ugly head.

My goal here is to show from different angles (see the tables below) how we can also rethink Western philosophy, not by new logical arguments, but by changing the parameters of what counts as an argument – once talking and thinking are seen as external and not existing in some netherworld.

Perhaps the key guiding points from all the preceding chapters are these:

- The reality of acting in the world has to do with relationships of doing things and having effects, which is usually certain 'knowledge', even though we might fail when recording or reporting the events.
- The reality of words and language has only to do with the brute effects on relationships with people and between people, and if we do not report those social relationships we have failed in our recording or reporting of them.
- The relations therefore between words and things always go through social relationships (the second virtual reality machine) and therefore can never be certain 'knowledge' – this has been the futile quest of Western philosophy, trying to make a certain or verifiable link

Table 5.2 Previous (incorrect) philosophical separations of things, people, and intervening activities with examples

Things	*People*	*Intervening activities*
	An example	
A cat	A speaker of or listener to the words 'cat', 'neko', 'gato', etc.	Saying or writing the words 'cat', 'neko', 'gato', etc.
Some previous terms used in philosophy and social sciences		
Things	Men	Intervening interpretive activity
Physical object	Image or idea	Words that denote those ideas or images
Referent	Thought or reference	Symbol
Thing	Mind	Sign
Designatum	Speaker	Sign
Designatum	Interpreter/interpretant	Sign vehicle
Objects and events	Talking and thinklings	Language

between saying something and the objects or events that we seem to be referring to.

To take this further and get the reader thinking differently from new angles, I first want to utilize and expand upon a scheme introduced by Arthur F. Bentley (1945). Bentley made this scheme following Peirce in pointing out three foci around which metaphysics has traditionally been built – what Bentley called *things*, *men*, and *intervening interpretive activity*, roughly corresponding also to objects, people, and language use. Examples of these three foci are the thing, mind, and sign of Lewis, the referent, thought, and symbol of Ogden and Richards, and the designatum, interpreter, and sign vehicle of Morris (Bentley, 1945). Table 5.2 has some examples from past philosophies.

To get the next perspective, we can put these together with the brute facts argument of Chapter 3. I suggest that philosophers and others have always talked about these three foci as separate only because they have incorrectly assumed that there are three different types of brute facts about these foci:

- Things seem to be separate metaphysical events because of the brute facts arguments I outlined earlier (like being hit by a brick) – these brute facts are typically about things we cannot do or change.
- The men (people, speakers, or interpreters in Table 5.2) have been assumed to be metaphysically separate because we are animate

creatures with a skin who move freely about the environment, and appear perceptually distinct from the rest of the cosmos – these brute facts are typically about things we can do (Bentley, 1941a, 1941b).

- Finally, and what is most relevant here, while intervening activities have sometimes been seen as having different brute events because they appear different – the sign is not the thing, a picture of a cat is not a cat – both philosophy and common sense have always confused the two. Two examples of this are: the brute event about a sentence "This dog is blue" is whether or not there is a blue dog there; "The dog is blue" is said to be true iff the dog is blue.

These are summarized in Table 5.3.

Some pragmatisms get close to this, but, as I have already tried to indicate above, it is because pragmatisms have not identified the brute events of words correctly that the relativism arises. Instead, I argued in Chapter 3 that words just have effects on appropriately trained people, and that is all they do, no different in principle from there being effects of being hit by a piece of wood. The relativism and misinterpretation of words is equivalent to the vagaries and vicissitudes of training listeners precisely.

The present argument can also show more clearly, though, how pragmatisms can be considered anti-dualisms, once the brute events of words are sorted out. In the arguments given here, considered again in terms of Bentley's scheme of things, speakers, and interpretive activities (Bentley, 1945), I have collapsed both speakers and, more importantly, interpretive activities into *things getting done*. All three are just examples of things getting done with the same brute events as 'things', excepting that speakers move about within what appears to be a self-contained skin, and excepting that interpretive activities only do things to people, not to non-people things or to non-trained people.

With this we can now get another perspective on the famous Western metaphysical dualisms. The consequence is that these dualisms only arose in the first place because of the common-sense (but false) separations between these three foci; from common sense distinctions between (what seemed to be) three distinguishable types of brute event in the world. If the three are considered separate, as they have been by both Western metaphysics and common sense, then the distinction between each pair constitutes a source of various dualisms. This has historically produced three (artificial) pairs of dualisms in philosophy, summarized in Table 5.4.

First, if *things* and *people* are separated, on the erroneous basis of their having different metaphysical brute events, then this constitutes

Table 5.3 The sources for believing (incorrectly) that different brute events can separate three metaphysical domains

Things as brute events
Usually the things I cannot do
I cannot walk through walls
My cat bit me
I eat food
People as brute events
Usually the things I can do and I seem to control
I walk to the store
I write words down
I talk to you
Intervening activities as brute events
According to both traditional Western philosophy and common sense
It is the same as the things denoted by the words ('things' above)
For example, the brute events about saying or thinking "The cat is eating" is whether or not a cat is eating
For example, Tarksi, "The cat is eating" is true or brute iff the cat is eating
But according to the present view (the second virtual reality machine)
The brute events about saying or thinking "The cat is eating" are what people do when I say this (and therefore equivalent to the first category above), not whether a cat is eating or whether anything 'catish' is even nearby, although empirically this is often the case

the traditional mind/body dualism – there are speakers' bodies (the 'thing' part of people) that move about and there are other things. The world is seen as separate from our bodies. This further promotes inner/outer dualisms, with an outer body and an inner speaker who does the intervening activities. It also promotes a behavior/environment split, such that behaviors are somehow split from their environments (Lee, 1992). In these ways, the skin assumes a metaphysical importance way beyond its dermal capabilities (Bentley, 1941a, 1941b).

Second, if *things* and *intervening activities* (talking, thinklings) are considered separate, then traditional dualisms of denotation and reference arise. There are things and there are words (cat and 'cat'), and the truth (brute reality) must surely be a correspondence between the two. Note that trying to bring these two together again after they were falsely split apart has been the bread-and-butter of Western philosophy.

Finally, separating *people* from the *intervening activities* has led to dualisms of people-as-machines versus people-as-minds or consciousness. It has raised (artificial) problems of how brains can know and how brains can be minds. It has led to positing the intervening activities as existing in Platonic realms of ideas, as a consciousness, and as biological programs in the brain, and it has led to the placement of knowledge into a fictitious 'knower' (Dewey & Bentley, 1949).

Table 5.4 Three types of dualism artificially produced by treating the three brute facts as metaphysically separate

Separating things and people (= Knowing how)
Traditional problems
Mind/body split
Absent and imaginary objects and their status
Behavior/environment split
People as merely mechanisms
Animal 'awareness'
Inner and outer events and what these mean; the behavioral superfice (Bentley)
Private events
Attempts to overcome the problems created
Bentley's skin argument and transdermality
Dewey and Bentley's transactionalism
Kantor's field ideas and other monisms
Separating things and intervening activities
Traditional problems
Denotation and reference
The truth of propositions
Absent and imaginary objects
Scientific verification
Attempts to overcome the problems created
Quine's indeterminacy thesis
Continental philosophy solutions leading Heidegger, Derrida, and others to strike out ~~words~~ so as to deny their import
'Cultural relativity' and postmodern attempts to ignore things, so that words become everything (e.g. Sartwell)
Separating people and intervening activities (= knowing that)
Traditional problems
How can a body/mind know?
The *cogito*
Nature of concepts and thoughts
Existence of Platonic ideas
Language acquisition and generatively
Saussure's independent *la langue*
Existence of biological language centers
Relation between knowledge and knower
Attempts to overcome the problems created
Dewey and Bentley's removal of a knower
Some continental philosophies' removal of a knower or author
Skinner's verbal behavior
Chomsky's deep and surface structure and LAD
Cognitive representations
Methodological behaviorisms, which try to ignore the intervening activities

More famously, this third separation was the birthplace of the *cogito*: "How do I know that I (as a person) exist?" – answer, by the different 'brute fact' that I think (intervening activity). We have already seen that the conception of the *cogito* arose from confusing perceptual and observational doubt with doubts about whether words can really correspond to things. If words or intervening activities cannot be perfectly shown to correspond to things, then this applies even to the 'things' about myself (the person or body). So the person, speaker, or body is written off as doubtful for the same reason as the rest of the environment, and then the *cogito* is supposed to rescue the situation by being unable to doubt the intervening activity to the same extent. Descartes' arguments for this last part are actually dubious, that we cannot doubt that our intervening activities could not exist, but that was Descartes' conclusion that led to having everything exist again.

So we can see from this perspective that the major dualisms in Western philosophy arose out of a tripartite division that was based on common-sense distinctions based on purported metaphysical differences in brute events. Pragmatism and other recent European philosophies have put the speaker or person-as-body into the 'things' category with wood and chairs, and have shown that the intervening activities cannot be defined by any correspondence to 'thing' brute events, but they have left those intervening activities (talking and thinking) in a netherworld by not reaffirming how they actually get a bruteness equivalent to that of things. By leaving this part out, the intervening activities were still present but with nothing to prevent or restrict them; words could do anything, and everything exists only because of words. It is true, then, that pragmatism only goes half-way and can rightly be accused of crude postmodernism and relativism, the ideas respectively that words are everything there is and that no words have any more or less effect than any other.

What I hope this shows is that the rethinking embodied in this book also allows us to explain and to correct previous philosophical conceptualizations that have led to the perennial issues and conundrums of Western philosophy. To help with this, in the Appendix I have summarized more succinctly the points that have been made.

How should we understand people?

At the beginning of this chapter I gave a breezy version of how we might start rethinking and understanding people and what they do. In final summary, it seems to me that there are a few key points that are the most difficult to rethink. I think it is worth restating them so that the reader can see the different ways I have tried to give new metaphors to change these. There will be many other ways to rethink, and hopefully you will come up with others.

What you do with all this once you rethink is not like embracing a singular new theory or foundation. Many ways of studying, understanding, and changing people can come from these rethinkings. I have my own that I discuss elsewhere, but I know there will be other, and probably better, ways to move on.

The most difficult rethinkings seem to be these:

- All people-events are controlled by external contexts even while involving brains and body and gooey stuff.
- Language use, talking, and thinking are controlled externally also.
- Language use is controlled only by the past and present effects that occur from people (trained speakers).
- All events occur 100 percent and what seem to be exceptions are really only so in talking and thinking.
- We must observe and measure all the contexts as far as possible, using appropriate methods.
- Making observational mistakes, not observing long enough, and observing the context poorly should not be mistaken for anything metaphysical or essential.
- Events can influence us without our seeing particles in between.
- We do not need to explicate the particle-chains between events.

I hope that in rethinking in these ways, or even in trying to rethink in these ways, you can gain some new understandings of how people – and you – work in this world and do the things we do.

References

Adams, D., & Lloyd, J. (1983). *The meaning of liff*. London: Pan Books.

Bentley, A. F. (1935). *Behavior knowledge fact*. Bloomington, IN: Principia Press.

Bentley, A. F. (1941a/1975). The human skin: Philosophy's last line of defense. In A. F. Bentley, *Inquiry into inquiries: Essays in social theory*. Westport, CT: Greenwood Press.

Bentley, A. F. (1941b). The behavioral superfice. *Psychological Review*, 48, 39–59.

Bentley, A. F. (1945). On a certain vagueness in logic. I. *Journal of Philosophy*, 42, 6-27.

Dewey, J., & Bentley, A. F. (1949). *Knowing and the known*. Boston: Beacon Press.

Freud, S. (1915/1984). *The unconscious* (Penguin Freud Library Vol. 11). London: Penguin Books.

Gibson, J. J. (1979). *An ecological approach to visual perception*. Boston: Houghton Mifflin.

Guerin, B. (forthcoming). *Understanding people through social contextual analysis: A practical guide*. Abingdon: Routledge.

Herbert, F. (1984). *Heretics of Dune*. London: New English Library.

Lao Tzu (1944). *Tao Te Ching*. Translated by Witter Bynner. Found on website: *Tao Te Ching* (175-plus translations of chapter 1). http://www.bopsecrets.org/gateway/passages/tao-te-ching.htm.

Lee, V. L. (1992). Transdermal interpretation of the subject matter of behavior analysis. *American Psychologist*, 47, 1337–1343.

Reps, P. (1957). *Zen flesh, Zen bones*. Harmondsworth, Middlesex: Penguin Books.

Appendix: tractatus psychologica

The real	*Notes*
There is a real world, and real things happen.	Friends and family die, and no amount of anything can bring them back to interact with us. Someone lets down the tires on your car and you cannot magically make them as they were.
There is utter realism in this. Not pragmatism. Not empiricism.	Pragmatism and empiricism are both to do with trying to find a (misguided) certainty in words.
Separating realism from words is the difficult part.	If you doubt this, allow me to slash the tires of your car and tell yourself it did not happen.
On the other hand, whatever we talk about is not real in any of the usual brute ways defined by philosophers.	I can talk about my car tires magically reappearing as they were prior to slashing. I can talk and say that my friend is no longer dead. I can talk about a big pink polka-dot spaceship appearing in front of me and relaying stories about Elvis to me.
Words do not *communicate* anything; they do not *express* anything; they do not *represent* anything; they do not *refer to* anything.	
There is utter unrealism in anything to do with the usual ways of thinking about words.	*The Way you can call Way is not the perennial way.* *The name you can name is not the perennial name.* (Lao Tzu)
Words do have real effects but we will get to that later and it will not be about communicating, expressing, representing, or referring.	A lot of time has been wasted pondering what my talking about aliens and Elvis is *really* communicating, expressing, representing, or referring to.

The real	*Notes*
So whatever happens, happens 100 percent; it is either happening or it is not. There are no probabilities in the world. There are no half-events in the world. All these 'exist' only in our ways of speaking, in words.	Anything against this is using words but treating them as real brute events in themselves – a mistake.
Two things seem to go against this:	
First, we can make mistakes in observing. But with repeated and multiple persons observing we do not make too many mistakes (contextual observation).	A lot of psychology and philosophy has assumed cross-sectional or brief observations as satisfactory.
If you only observe and participate by having three old, blind men investigate rapidly on your behalf then you are going to make many mistakes – you are asking for trouble! You should observe over time, not in cross-sections.	*If observation were confined to what one pair of eyes can see at one instant, the criticism would hold. But such a position is absurd. Following it back, one would be compelled to pass further to elements of isolated sense determination, and would not 'see' anything at all. We never 'see' more than one side of the elephant at once, but we regard him as 'wholly' visible, as observable objectively in a frame of visibility. We can turn him around, or, more readily, walk around him, and make our verifications. The elephant that confronts scientific investigation and practical observation alike is the full object, and not an instantaneous, partial sense-report.* (Bentley, 1935, pp. 213–14)
Second, because talking is utter unrealism (in the normal sense), it is possible to talk about events as having less than 100 percent probability of happening. It depends a lot on how big we talk – minute little details (relative to our bodies) or huge events over time (history). None of what we talk about is real in the four usual ways, so it does not matter that we have half-events and non-events being talked about. That is not where their brute reality lies.	Talking does have a 'truth' or reality but that is something else altogether to get to below.

The real	*Notes*
Just as probabilities are not real except in talking, so too causes. Events happen as a mixture of other events (their contexts) and arise or emerge when things are mixed in the right combination. To understand events we need to find out the combination of other events we must combine. With language we often pick out one or two of these contextual events (the most salient during observation, usually, or the most speakable) and call them causes. But this is utter unrealism again.	
If there is to be a notion of 'truth' then it is just about: *What gets done in what contexts.*	• Not *whether it gets done* (correspondence to a prior verbal activity) • Not *how it got done* (by referencing it to verbal causes and theories) • Not *whether it was effective* (effective in getting something else done we can name, or survival, or utility) • Not *how we talk about the events later* (correspondence to other verbal theories and hypotheses)
The reality of using language	
Language is truly a veil of Maya that wraps over all events as we live, and it leads us to act as if some unreal was real. Having this veil of illusion can be useful, however. Virtual realities are useful.	Although not in the way that Advaita Vedanta philosophy would have it.
Slashing with a knife will destroy a car tire. It happens. But that sentence is still just words. If I slash a car tire with a knife and it does not cut it, that event is not somehow less than 100 percent real. It is still 100 percent real (presuming I have observed well). It is only my words (if you still trust them to reflect the real) that make it look as if what I did with the knife was less than 100 percent. Even if I slash a peach with a knife and it does not cut. Just because I *say* it *has to* cut it does nothing to the reality of what happens.	But my talk about probability affects listeners 100 percent and does not have partial effects.

The real	*Notes*
The biggest problem in the history of psychology (and philosophy before that) has been accepting passively or acquiescing in the common ways of talking about 'psychological' events.	
My definition of psychology is that it is the academic repository for *events involving people for which the majority of the contextual events are hidden from us in some way.*	And this does not mean hidden 'inside' the head! Those 'hidden events' are social and external, as we will see.
Hence psychology is a dumping ground for events with difficult-to-see contexts. "I cannot see a cause for this event so it must be something 'psychological'." This has made it difficult, of course, and there is no blame.	
So the brute reality of any and all events is that they have effects, consequences, and do things for other events.	Talk and thinking are clearly examples of those events, but their brute reality does not lie in 'correctly' representing, referring to, expressing, or communicating those realities.
The question then is: What is the reality, as cannot be told, of language? This becomes a question of: What effects or consequences does language use have in the world?	In what ways is the use of language part of contexts that move through happenings and events?
First, language does not affect anything that seems to be *referred* to.	Saying 'cat' does not directly affect any cat. Although, in a very different sense than we are talking about, the air from loudly saying 'cat' might scare a cat as part of contexts.
Second, language use only has effects by affecting people, not other objects.	Language only 'works' on people; language only has a reality by the effects we observe it having on people.
Two caveats: (1) Talking to yourself is a very special and important category, dealt with below. (2) It is often difficult to observe the effects of language use but we can observe all the contexts around it over a longer time if we get rid of our blind old elephant-men. But language only affects people if you include yourself in that.	

The real	*Notes*
Third, language is artificial and is only effective in contexts that involve trained people. But it is also very effective behavior if those people have been trained previously or have a history.	Saying 'cat' to a person who can only speak Euskara has no effect beyond what a puff of air might have for a cat.
The 'meaning' of a word, if we still want to use that way of speaking, is not its *use* but its *social training and history*.	To explicate the definition of a word or phrase we must explicate the social training of the speaker and listener.
If we want a word to only have effects ('have meaning') in a very specific context, then we must deal with training issues, not learning to describe an abstract 'meaning'.	If we wanted 'cat' to only and ever be used in the context of very dark orange felines of a certain size and only those with black ears, then we would need a rigorous training program, not a dictionary.
So the 'meaning' of a word or sentence depends on the context, the audiences, and the history of the audiences.	
Obviously there will therefore be huge variations in what happens when someone says something, and handling this is a ubiquitous social strategy. Misunderstanding is rife.	So the 'meaning' of talking about "a big pink polka-dot spaceship appearing in front of me and relaying stories about Elvis to me" is purely in the effects that has on the audiences, which will be hugely variable. It can include future avoidance, being wary in future of the speaker, locking them away, or laughing at them or with them.
All the effects of language depend on the more specific contexts and audiences and the histories or training of those audiences. If you want the same effects on all audiences, in all contexts, then you need to do a lot of training or restrict the audiences you talk with.	Cult groups and academic disciplines know about this. Only dictators and despots will be able to implement accurate dictionaries.
The contexts for action to emerge are outside of us in our surrounding contexts.	Including the historical contexts that brought us here to be as we are now.

The real	*Notes*
The contexts of events that bring about our actions do not originate inside our heads. The inside of our heads clearly are involved in such actions, but if you look in there, even closely, there are no originators. There is murky, bloody stuff. So-called decisions do not spontaneously happen but occur because of the way that contexts have moved and shaped us like plasticine.	Volcanoes erupt when a certain combination of contexts is in place (albeit very complex and very difficult for scientists to observe). That confluence of contexts is shaped or arranged gradually over time from other events. When the confluence of contexts brings about a sudden eruption it is not because some hidden element in the ground suddenly 'decided' to spurt. It spurts from the arrangement of contexts that have been shaped. There is no decision-making.
Likewise for us. When we start walking to the shops we have not 'made a decision', even an 'unconscious' one, to go to the shops. Events have been gradually arranged by other events such that we go to the shops. How we talk and explain will be different, but that depends on our social relationships to listeners.	
This is very difficult for us to understand, however, because of the complex way that language forms part of those contexts, and the social arrangements that language use always implies.	

Reference

Bentley, A. F. (1935). *Behavior knowledge fact*. Bloomington, IN: Principia Press.

Index